SAY IT AGAIN

an autobiography (in sonnets)

Volume 1: The Road Goes Away
(the first thirty years) 1942-1972

by Michael Lally

Beltway
EDITIONS

Some of these poems have appeared in magazines and other poetry collections, too many to list but I thank all the editors and publishers of those publications, including Dan Simon, Bob Hershon, Dick Lourie, Mark Pawlak, Paul Portuges, John Martin, Jim Haining; and Indran Amirthanayagam and Sara Cahill Marron of Beltway Editions for *Say It Again*.

Also thanks always for their love and support to my children Caitlin Lally Hotaling, Miles Lally, and Flynn Lally. And special thanks for their support of *Say It Again* to Karen Allen, Michael O'Keefe, Susan Campbell, John Restivo, Daniel Purkis, Beth Joselow, Tom Mandel, and most of all to my dear and closest friend and confidante: Terence Winch.

www.beltwayeditions.com

Printed in the United States of America
10 9 8 7 6 5 4 3 2 1

Book Design: Jorge Ureta Sandoval
Cover design by Susan Campbell.
Cover photograph of Michael Lally by Len Randolph, 1972.
ISBN: 978-1-957372-06-8

Beltway Editions (www.beltwayeditions.com)
4810 Mercury Drive
Rockville, MD, 20853
Indran Amirthanayagam: Publisher
Sara Cahill Marron: Publisher

“…the voice on the
phone from West Orange saying love the
first time saying What saying Wait saying
Say it again…”

from *South Orange Sonnet 19*

Table of Contents

Introduction: The Poetry of Michael Lally

It's a commonplace that the two great literary subjects of the 20th century were sex and the self. I think of Michael Lally as a Beat poet, essentially, devoted to the investigation of the self and of sexuality in the context of everything. His work as a whole may be read as an ongoing autobiography, the confessions of an American poet. It is revealing, often raw, full of self-mythologizing, self-praise, self-doubt, attitude, discourse, speculation, exhortation, and a whole lot more. The last book that I read of Michael's is *Of*, a book-length (100 pages) poem, which reminded me of another commonplace, this one about novelists: that the novelist brings to each novel everything they know and think and feel about the world, and that they embark on a journey during which they will learn more. *Of* seemed not just a re-statement of previous material, or an extension of familiar themes, although it was both of those, but a new hazard. I do not intend to attempt to tell you Michael's life-story, because the definitive version is available in his work. Visit his blog (lallysalley.blogspot.com) and you will be able to make your own discoveries.

In fact, I believe that the very best introduction to Michael is the anthology he edited, *None of the Above: New Poets of the USA*, published by The Crossing Press in Trumansburg, New York, 1976. It contains work by 31 poets: Maureen Owen, Darrell Gray, Ed Cox, Bruce Andrews, Robert Slater, Merrill Gilfillan, David Drum, Philip Lopate, Ron Silliman, Joe Brainard, Bernadette Mayer, Dave Morice, George Mattingly, Joanne Kyger, Ray Di Palma, Patti Smith, Jim Gustafson, Nathan Whiting, Terence Winch, Joe Ribar, Hilton Obenzinger, Lynne Dreyer, Michael Lally, P. Inman, Simon Schuchat, Barbara Baracks, Tim Dlugos, Lorenzo Thomas, Paul Violi, Paula Novotnik, Alice Notley.

There were poets in there I'd never heard of. One or two of them I still haven't heard of. It was a wholly eclectic selection, reflecting Michael's populist approach to everything, including poetics. There were some jokes at Michael's expense a few years ago about his claiming to have started "language poetry"—I don't know that anyone believed that he had made such a claim in any seriousness, but the fact is that six of the poets included in Ron Silliman's anthology, *In the American Tree* (1986) were in *None of the Above*: Silliman, Andrews, Mayer, Di Palma, Dreyer, and Inman. Three of them were included in Douglas Messerli's much less expansive *"Language" Poetries* (1987): Di Palma, Inman, and Andrews. The fact is that Michael was supporting what would become the "Language Poetry movement" at its onset, and I wouldn't be surprised if *None of the Above* was the first anthology in which these poets were published together. There were six poets associated with DC in the anthology: Cox, Winch, Dreyer, Lally, Inman, and Dlugos. There was Patti Smith, prior to her music career taking off. There was Joanne Kyger, an associate of the Beats and the California Renaissance. I had been in love with Joanne Kyger since I'd read *Descheo Notebook* in 1971. The main reason I might have regretted not having done enough to warrant possible inclusion in *None of the Above* was that I might have been published with Joanne Kyger and my

DC friends. Not that the rest of the company was too shabby. However, my first point is this: Michael's identity extends in all kinds of directions. This anthology reflects his social and political inclinations, as well as his literary interests. And this really was alternative poetry, of many different kinds. Most of the poets in *None of the Above* would have been extremely unlikely candidates for publication by any of the mainstream publishing houses and presses. My second point is that *None of the Above* contains Michael's poem "My Life," i.e., his signature as well as his life story to that point, his poetics and his science, his money and his mouth.

Michael is an actor, too (under the name Michael David Lally, due to SAG restrictions). He's been in a bunch of movies and a good deal of television shows, including *LA Law, NYPD Blue* and *Law & Order*. My favorite work of his so far was in *NYPD Blue*, second season, episode 16, "UnAmerican Graffiti," in which he played an artist who agreed to testify against some very bad people after witnessing a violent crime. I didn't have to look it up. I have the DVD. His Walter Hoyt is an unforgettable character, with a convincingly distracted demeanor, explaining his sense of aesthetics to the cops, and then having a huge amount of moral fiber and fortitude. It was very gratifying to see an artist not portrayed as a buffoon, but as a genuinely heroic character. Henry Fonda heroic, not Bruce Willis heroic. There was an excellent 1997 follow-up episode featuring the same character: *NYPD Blue*, Season 4, Episode 10, "My Wild Irish Nose." Michael also had a great bit at the end of the first *Deadwood* series.

Anyway, Michael is a performer. He's an actor, he's a performance-oriented reader, and he's a performance-oriented writer. Every poem is a performance. Every poem is Michael interacting with his own domain, his connections, his history, his psyche, his ego, his mood, his karma, you name it. What drives him there drives him in the world at large. Whatever that is, it's the same thing that made him such a force in the DC poetry scene in the 1970s.

I didn't spend that much time around Michael during my first year in Washington, 1973–74. It was clear that the radical spirit of the 1960s was thriving still during that time around the Dupont Circle scene, and that there was a huge amount of energy coming out of the alternative poetry community in particular. Michael was at the center of that. He and Terence Winch were the driving forces of Mass Transit and SOUP, with Lee Lally and Ed Cox in support. One of their most important endeavors was the reading series at the Pyramid Gallery across the street from the Community Bookstore on "P" Street, but closer to 21st Street. I did my first-ever reading in America at that gallery, Sunday, January 26, 1975, with Paul Violi.

Lally and Winch were Li Po & Tu Fu, Abbott & Costello, Slim 'n' Slam, Ginsberg & Kerouac, Starsky & Hutch, Ren & Stimpey, all rolled into one duo. Aside from Ed Cox, Tim Dlugos, Peter Inman, and Lynne Dreyer, other DC poets such as Beth Joselow, Tina Darragh, Bernard Welt, and Phyllis Rosenzweig received early support and encouragement from Michael and/or Terence, as did many other poets. Of course, there were plenty of conflicts, issues, disagreements, etceteras, during this era, and Michael was often at the center of them. Issues of power and perceived power always cause divisiveness, even in regard to poetry publications, reading opportunities, and so on. And, also, this was the time in which ideas of "political correctness" (as we now know it) were being formulated. I don't mean "political correctness" in terms of the zealous application of the letter of the law, as it is now interpreted very often. I mean ideas regarding appropriate behavior, attitudes, and speech, receiving serious consideration and attention. There were always differences in opinion about this, about what was right, about what was the right application, about a lot of things. Everything in the garden was not always lovely. Differences about these things sometimes escalated into personal animosities. Michael was no saint and he did not enjoy universal approval within his own community. And there were some "mainstream" poets, and some poets who were not attached to either the mainstream or the alternative communities, who regarded Michael (and others in the Dupont Circle gang) with hostility. As the 1970s progressed, I found myself to be the subject of this hostility by association, sometimes. Aside from whatever hostility I might have earned directly, that is.

Michael has always been very generous. He has always made things happen. He has made many good things happen for a lot of people, including myself. And he is an amazingly prolific writer. Some of his very early writing was what might be termed experimental, more so than his signature work, which was well established by 1972, when SOUP published *The South Orange Sonnets.* His signature work was distinct, and remains so. The experimental edge did not disappear from his work. It simply became part of his style of writing, and part of his persona as a poet. A more realized version of that style developed between *The South Orange Sonnets* (1972) and *Rocky Dies Yellow* (1975), that was very much his own, very clear and recognizable. Its apotheosis was "My Life" (1975).

The language in *The South Orange Sonnets* went beyond the vernacular into a kind of anti-literary version of American speech, and the attitudes it expressed were defiant, in-your-face, and provocative. The language reminded me of what the great American novelist James Jones had devised for his novel, *From Here to Eternity*, an approximation of raw speech, although

Jones's language represented a particular subculture (the US military), while Michael's represented his own New Jersey roots and identity. *The South Orange Sonnets* was an unflinching portrait of Michael's social context, in which his persona emerged in the form of voice and posture.

The cover of *Rocky Dies Yellow* shows a still from the 1938 movie, *Angels with Dirty Faces*; the young street punks who would later become the Bowery Boys are contemplating a newspaper headline announcing the death of James Cagney's Rocky Sullivan, an Irish American, New York City hood. And it's all there. Just as the cover of *The South Orange Sonnets* depicted Michael's social roots, the cover of *Rocky* depicted his true cultural roots: the movies in general and Cagney in particular. One high literary effort to accommodate Michael's work named him the American François Villon, but, no, he was poetry's Cagney, poetry's Bowery Boy, a fast-talking Irish American tough guy. This was not simply a matter of Michael finding his "voice" in the traditional, literary sense. Michael was an actor long before he was cast in the low-budget horror movie, *The Nesting* (1981), featuring John Carradine and Gloria Grahame. He was a natural actor. What Michael did was create the perfect role for himself: himself, out of Cagney and company, out of the autobiographical traditions of the Beat Generation, and out of his counterculture experiences. This was an authentic, postmodern moment. The counterculture aspect related to another aspect of *Rocky Dies Yellow*: "The meaning of that title and cover for me was that, like Cagney's Rocky Sullivan, I was pretending to be softer and less macho than I thought I really was, so that my kids and all kids wouldn't grow up like we did, with all that tough guy model shit, but instead would be more sensitive to women and gays etc. etc. In other words, the times in which most of *Rocky* was written, were when feminism and 'gay revolution' were first having an impact on me and those I knew." This "softer" side was evident in the lyrical tendencies of Michael's work, also.

There is so much material that I could write about. I am extremely partial to the two chapbooks Tina Darragh published in her Dry Imager Production series, *Malenkov Takes Over* and *Oomaloom*. *Malenkov* is a twofer, with Tina's *My First Play* starting at one end and *Malenkov Takes Over* at the other, collages in both cases, collage as writing, writing as collage, image as word, word as image. Very cool. Also very cool, *Oomaloom*, a book of prose, autobiography, poetics, and counterculture history, containing Michael's famous "The Dress Incident." Tina Darragh is the greatest publisher ever.

In the Mood is another favorite, and not only because I was one of its publishers, along with Diane Ward, Bernard Welt, and our fearless leader, Terence Winch, all of us editors of Titanic Books. *In the Mood* could have been called "My Poetics." It's a tribute to Frank O'Hara. The Titanic edition has a fabulous front cover designed by me. Xeroxed-down-to-pixels photograph of O'Hara, smudgy rubber stamp work for the author's name and title. Wow.

Some good places to start reading Michael's work would be *Hollywood Magic*, published by Dennis Cooper's Little Caesar in 1982 and containing a lot of poems, including "My Life," and *Cant Be Wrong*, published by Allan Kornblum's Coffee House Press in 1996, also containing a lot of poems, including "Where Do We Belong" a long poem about Michael's return to Ireland and his clan's roots, a poem which he also reads on his *What You Find There* CD. But, really, the Lally oeuvre is outré in all directions, so it's all win-win.

One of Michael's strengths as an actor and as a reader is his voice. Besides *What You Find There*, there's a recording of a reading Michael gave at the West End Bar, NYC, March 12, 1978, at pennsound (along with the material that's on the CD): http://writing.upenn.edu/pennsound/x/Lally.html

Michael's long poem *March 18, 2003* has been described as the greatest poem of our time. Michael read the poem at The Great Hall at Cooper Union on Tuesday, Feb 20th, 2007, prior to a talk by Howard Zinn, to an audience of a thousand plus. Bob Holman introduced Michael as "Whitman to Zinn's Lincoln" (the podium at Cooper Union is the one where Lincoln gave his great anti-slavery address): "As a poet, a fearless, edgy poet, Michael Lally has been giving readers his version of history for the past 35 years. He has done so with the political forthrightness and performance punch of Ginsberg, with the wit and language skills of O'Hara. But because of the place of poetry in this country, a bard like Lally, while a member of the Pantheon to all manner of poets, remains unknown to the public at large, even an audience like tonight's cognoscenti." Michael's reading was a huge success.

The most crucial period of Michael's development as a poet was spent in DC, and the impact of his presence here is still an ongoing reality, as are the benefits (for so many) that resulted from his presence and his activities. As far as "alternative poetry" is concerned, no city outside of New York and San Francisco can rival the achievements of the poets of Washington in terms of publications and reading series, and general ambience. Poets in their twenties, thirties, and forties associated with DC are the beneficiaries of that prestige, as well as being the creators of its continuation. Michael was there at the beginning, and, for those who care about these things, he deserves the highest regard.

—Doug Lang

[posted at at 3:47 AM Thursday, August 9, 2007 at http://douglangsdcpoetryblog.blogspot.com/search/label/poets]

Editor's note: Doug Lang (1941–2022) was a Welsh-American poet who lived his last 50 years in Washington, DC, where, like Michael Lally, he was a catalyst of major impact on the region's literary scene. He ran an influential reading series that paired visiting luminaries with local writers, started several small presses and magazines, and taught writing (among other subjects) at the Corcoran College of Art for 37 years. Lang's own writing, characterized by his extraordinary creative energy and linguistic inventiveness, is only now starting to receive the recognition it deserves. Michael Lally and Doug Lang were good friends for many years. This introduction is adapted from a blog post Lang wrote in 2007, but his insights into Lally's writing are as penetrating and insightful now as they were then.

AUTHOR'S NOTE

THE SOUTH ORANGE SONNETS were written in the 1960s with some recent revisions, the other sonnets constructed from writing back then, and the years since. I often recycle images and lines and observations in my work to see how they ride in different contexts, but every section of this volume is newly complete with many details checked against journal entries, letters, newspapers, flyers, and the memories of others. But in the end I relied mostly on my own memories. The language and perspective are meant to partly match the times written about, not the times they were written in.

PROLOGUE

My father's cronies called him Jimmy and me Little Jimmy even though I told them over and over MY NAME'S MICHAEL! I was the youngest of seven, one of them already named James. When the oldest became a Franciscan friar, all the neighborhood ladies and nuns at school constantly asked me Are you going to be a priest like your brother? Which I would say No no no to. I never wanted to be mistaken for anyone else. I planned to make my mark on the world so my name would forever be distinct, and at the sound of it multitudes would genuflect. Or the secular equivalent.

THE SOUTH ORANGE SONNETS

"It's like a man being born in a little place, just a bend in the road somewhere. After a while he begins to travel the road. He travels all the road there is and then he comes back. That man, he understands something when he gets back. He knows the road goes away and he knows the road comes back just the same way it goes away."

—Sidney Bechet

1

In books it was The Lackawana Valley.
The Lackawana Railroad ran through it
separating those on the hill from us.
Lackawana Place was the toughest block
in the neighborhood until 1952 when
the temptations and reputation moved
to Church Street where *THE PINK DEVILS*
had roses tattooed between their thumbs
and forefingers, wore delicate gold
crucifixes on chains around their
brown Italian necks, and carried porno
playing cards from Newark, the city
where parades got lost and statues
died. Newark, where we all had lived.

2

My brother brought the moon back from
Okinawa. I mean, there they learned of
the surrender three days late and then
they danced all night. My brother played
the saxophone. Junkman Willy did a one
step that most girls didn't want to do.
They called him that for all the old cars
he worked on til he was old enough to
drive. He was a paddy cat like me and we
lived on Cabbage Hill til we were old
enough to live anywhere. We believed
Italians and Jews ran *THE SYNDICATE*
maybe the world. In West Orange a man
hung himself higher than he could reach.

3

The girls liked to dance with Eddie
we believed. He came back from jail
with big muscles and, it was rumored
bleached blonde hair. He had a tattoo
with the name crossed out and dimples.
One girl's father sent Eddie to school
in Las Vegas to learn to be a shill.
The girl's father was a big man in Las
Vegas it was rumored. Eddie was a big
man in South Orange. While he was gone
I met an Italian girl with hair on her
chest and poured beer out my side of
Junkman's truck when nobody was looking.
After only two weeks Eddie came home.

4

In East Orange Carol Robinson decided I
was her boyfriend. Her father found out
before I did. Told his friends and neigh-
bors how he didn't want no white boy hang-
ing around his little girl. One asked me
not to pass the time at his house anymore
listening to his son's Clifford Browns or
talking to his twin daughters. Walking
home that night three teenagers sitting
on a stoop on Halstead Street yelled: Hey
white boy, whatchu doin aroun here? You
know where you are? Where you from? When
I answered South Orange this fat girl said
Shoot, that muss be Carol Rob's turkey.

5

Little Robert called himself a sporting man
at fourteen. Came by Charlie's house talking
about being a gambling fool and losing a
hundred dollars a minute and who has got
the playing cards. A friend of Charlie's wife
laughed and said Ain't you too old for card
games now? Charlie's wife made most men turn
around. When I was fourteen I watched her
walk by the store where I swept the floor.
Seven years later Charlie's cousin told me I
danced too close to Charlie's wife. My father
figured Charlie, Kenny, Bobby and the other
friends I loved were lazy cause they didn't
have good jobs. Kenny didn't even have a job.

6

In 1959 I thought of myself as *NEVER
FEAR* and liked to talk about a door
that when you walked through it you were
dancing. My father thought we had to be
up to no good out til two o'clock in the
morning. We rode around in Charlie's car
and talked. We decided one difference
between white girls and black girls was
the way you danced with them. White girls
you held around the waist with your right
arm. You put the same arm over a black
girl's shoulder. That was in 1959. Did you
ever have a woman's cunt wrapped around
your head asked Eddie. That was in 1956.

7

One year our people refused to buy Christmas
cards that said *SEASONS GREETINGS*. A year
later we christened the new homes on the hill
JEWSTEAD. Three years later we sang *Guns for
the Arabs, bicycles and sneakers for the Jews.*
Then a year came when the Jewish girls turned
soft and ripe and full of round things we
longed to hold. That was the year we all wanted
to be Jewish. We wanted to kiss the thing
they hung on their doors. We wanted to dip
our fingers into whatever holy water was theirs.
But most of all we didn't want to wait to be
the forbidden goyim they would sneak down
from their hill three years later to sample.

8

A sign across the street said *WATCH
CHILDREN* The street ended at the top
with the house where the man lived
who sang opera on his front stoop at
three or four in the morning when he
came home drunk. Sober he repaired
telephones. At the bottom it crossed
what passed for a highway in 1942
only to dead end into the railroad
tracks. It had fifteen houses on it
a bowling alley and diner and an
Esso gas station and a practice
football field where we played Ring-
a-lario the night Babe Ruth died.

9

When my mother died two Irish great aunts
came over from New York. The brassy one
wore her hat tilted and always sat with
her legs wide apart. At the wake she told
me loud You look like your grandfather
the cop if you ever get like him shoot
yourself. The other one waited til after
the funeral to pull my ear down to her
level and whisper You're a good looking
young man but if you don't shave off them
side boards people will mistake you for
a Puerto Rican. We had so many cousins
in our neighborhood everybody called my
mother Aunt Irene. Even the Italians.

10

My uncle shot himself before I was born.
My grandfather who carried an old petri-
fied potato in his pocket for his arthi-
ritis got up and walked out of the funeral.
His sons slipped out of their pews as
piously as they knew how and went to find
him. He was buttoning up his fly as they
came through the big oak doors of the
church and caught the reflection of the
sunlight on his piss. He used to open the
door of a fast moving vehicle which the
driver would hysterically beg to a stop
squeezing everything. He'd say It's time
to shake a little water off the potatoes.

11

In the morning people read *THE DAILY NEWS*
I pored over the cheesecake in the center
spread and in the newsreels in my head was
Eddie only more like me escorting one of
those women to the opening night of the in-
ternationally renowned BIG APPLE CLUB.
The older kids built their clubhouse in the
vacant lot where we played in the 1938 Olds
mobile with the miniature pin up of Betty
Grable in the suicide knob on the steering
wheel or in the open sewer we called The
Brook. One cousin made a coop for a sick
pigeon he was nursing. When the pigeon flew
away we made that coop our little clubhouse.

12

The Lackawana Railroad was an electric commuter
special that cut off the head of a ten year old
Boy Scout one summer. He was listening to the
tracks to hear if the train was coming. His
cousin saw it happen and was sick for a week.
He was seven. In bed when I was a kid listening
to the sound of the Lackawana rolling by I'd
dream of the places it would take me someday.
And it did. It took me to all the places it goes
to like Orange East Orange Maplewood Movies
Brick Church Newark and Hoboken. Sometimes
we jumped off halfway home to avoid paying.
One year somebody got a plate in his head from
jumping off onto something hard like my cousins.

13

Junkman was the oldest of fourteen kids. My father called him a bum when he quit school to work construction. My father quit school in 1912 to work in a hardware store. Junkmans younger brothers went to the Catholic Prep School. One was crushed by his locker his first year there and he died. A family of eleven lived on one side of us. Once my brother the cop pulled up to a couple in a car making out. He put his light on them and saw it was one of the girls next door. She was with another girl. When Junkman began his own construction company my father asked me why I wasn't ambitious like that.

14

The tree between the sidewalk and the curb attracted me. The leaves turning up in the breeze before a summer storm revealed a side that glowed, flashed like the palms of a dark woman shaping castles in the air. My father didn't like it. He'd ask why a boy sat on the stoop staring at trees when he could be watching TV learning the things a boy should know to be well liked by the men who could help him. Golfing terms, starting line ups, some news. Too much thinking can ruin you, he'd say. When we were alone my mother would ask Don't you think there might be something wrong with having no white friends.

15

My cousin was an artist but no one knew.
They thought he was only a work of art
like a pinball machine made of marble.
When someone deliberately broke the first
two letters of the ESSEX HOUSE sign, my
cousin did the same with a new kid's head.
He grew bigger than any cousin and more
gentle. Eddie no, I said, I never did
have a lady's cunt wrapped around my head.
I knew Eddie was an artist when he ate all
the aspirin. Girls from *THE KRAZY KITTENS*
played *EDDIE MY LOVE* eighteen times in a
row that night. Eddie looked at me and
said Whadja do, come out of a horses ass?

16

They say prospectors saved their scalps
by acting crazy. I acted as crazy as I
could when white guys asked me what it
was like with a, didn't want to say it
but afraid to look like they didn't want
to say it, said it: *nigger*. I hit them.
Or I told them Fine as 400 wine. Like
laying under that tree before a storm
watching the leaves turn over and shine.
Like getting it steady and nice. Like
the first time twice. Like standing in
the rain laughing. Like sitting at Broad
and Market, spitting at the moon and
hitting it. The word I wanted to marry.

17

There is some music you have to listen to.
In South Orange there were rich Catholics
rich Protestants and rich Jews. My cousin
became a cop. His brother was stabbed by
an Italian called Lemon Drop. Across the
street lived two brothers called Loaf and
Half a Loaf. My brother became a cop. On
St. Patrick's Day 1958 I came home drunk. My
mother said He's only fifteen. My father:
It had to happen once. My grandfather was
a cop. One cousin won a beauty contest at
thirteen. My sister married a cop. By 1959
I knew I was going to be a jazz musician.
My father joined AA before I was even born.

18

At first the world's great heroes were FDR
Churchill and Uncle Joe Stalin. The block
hero was *FLYING ACE* who shot down Krauts
on a seven inch screen. One brother served
with a Navy Band, one with the US Army
Air Corps. Before TV we sat through Sunday
matinees with newsreel footage of Nazi war
crimes. The boarder in our house had been
a dough boy in World War I. We called him
uncle. My third brother worked on tanks in
Germany during the Korean thing. I joined
the Air Force on February eighth 1962. I
went AWOL July fourth 1962. For a long time
no one we knew ever went away a civilian.

19

There were people who didn't need nick-
names. Love I'd say to myself walking
those streets under the old gas lights.
The woman on Valley Street who waited
after her friend went home. The eyes of
pretty Italian girls as their boyfriends
pulled up to the curb. The voice on the
phone from West Orange saying love the
first time saying What saying Wait saying
Say it again. Or like getting on the bus
to Newark six thirty in the morning
with a beautiful black girl in a party
dress and all the people going to work.
In 1960 you could star in South Orange.

20

My father lost the store, we all went to
work when I was ten. Then he became a
ward heeler. My grandfather was dead before
I knew he spoke Gaelic. My father could
remember when they had mules instead of
automobiles and you had to remove your cap
and step to the curb to let the rich walk
by. My grandfather was glad to die in the
USA. He'd say if you can't find a job within
thirty miles of New York City there aren't
any jobs to be found. My father would say
You can write all the poetry you want to
when you're a millionaire. Eddie would say
You got to try a shoe on before you buy it.

THE SAINT BONAVENTURE SONNETS

"The mind is like a parachute: it only functions when it's open."

—Jon Hendricks

1

My brother Buddy spent the end of WWII in
the Navy on Okinawa. Tommy on an Army
Air Corps base in the South, where he heard
the souls of Kamikaze pilots crying out to
him for help. After the war, he became Father
Campion, Franciscan missionary to Japan.
In 1960 he got me a family-of-a-friar scholarship
to Saint Bonaventure's, where he'd gone on
The GI Bill four years after Thomas Merton
wrote *SEVEN STORY MOUNTAIN* while
teaching there. The manuscript, a precious
relic under glass in the library, cried out to me
to preserve the record of my own life so far,
nine years later distilled into twenty sonnets.

2

The college was in Five Mile Valley on
the road to Olean, still scarred by The
Great Depression. My first stop: the radio
station, where I offered to sweep the floor.
They tested me on a microphone instead
and hired me as a d. j. for a jazz show, my
theme song a swinging, marching-band,
no-vocals *LOLLIPOP*, evoking my child-
hood nickname. Recently coed, with a
handful of girls, the few black students
were males and all on the basketball team.
Except for Tom Mosley, a freshman too,
who stuttered like a lot of black men from
the South did then, and I would later do.

3

Tom was from South Carolina. Smart, dark,
and good looking, he dressed more like
someone on their way to church than ready
to jump up on a bandstand and wail, like me,
when we ran in the black clubs around Olean.
My roommate, Marino Vincente, Champ to
his friends, a tough little Italian from Philly,
dug Sinatra as much as I did. Old friends
with Bobby Rydell, Champ took me to see
Rydell's show when it was in Buffalo, then
backstage to meet his neighborhood buddy,
whose real name, Champ said, was Riderelli.
My first time in a star's dressing room. Both
unexpectedly humble: the room and Rydell.

4

The son of a tailor, Champ taught me
how to care for my jazzman vines and
introduced me to James Joyce when he
couldn't make sense of the first page of
A PORTRAIT OF THE ARTIST AS A
YOUNG MAN, reading it aloud in be-
fuddled wonder. Despite the unfamiliar
words, their melody made sense to me.
I spent all night reading every page, each
revealing how to turn language into music
in ways I hadn't imagined possible before.
I'd been writing poetry and stories since
I first held a pen, but now began my first
novel to go along with the autobiography.

5

One October dinnertime, two seniors cleared a spot on a table in the dining hall and hoisted a man up onto it. It took a second to see he was the Democratic presidential nominee's little brother Bobby. Slight and seemingly shy, he exuded moral fervor as he railed against our enemies, or his, singling out the Teamsters. My cop brother Robert was a Teamster first, driving a truck for Ballantine Beer but quitting during a strike when his Teamster boss told him to break a scab's leg. As RFK finished, forelock hanging over his eyes, shirt marked by sweat, tie loose, like an Irish Sinatra, the place erupted in cheers. Any Nixon support disappeared in the outburst.

6

Linda, a milky-skinned townie ostracized for dating the very dark Big T, even though he was the star of the basketball team, and even after he dropped her, had platinum pixie hair, wore black cat's-eye glasses, and wept after too many beers, over the U.S. letting the Hungarian Freedom Fighters down. Joan, a pale senior with long straight black hair, unlike Jersey girls' high-rise hairdos that looked like they were designed by their own personal architects, gave me *A STONE FOR DANNY FISHER*, the novel *KING CREOLE* was based on, saying it reminded her of me. She drove a 1950, black, shoebox Ford we did a lot but not everything in.

7

Champ invited me to his row house in South
Philly for a weekend. His family welcoming, but
after knocking off a quart of beer with dinner
and later a pint of bourbon, I overheard them
whisper how typically Irish I was. Sam, Italian
too, was a senior who seemed much older with
his receding dark hair combed straight back
close to his head, old-man style. Shorter and
thicker than me, he could play his trumpet with
anybody, any time, in any tempo, and any key.
He always wore a long overcoat after the first
frost, which came early that far North, making
him look like a tree stump, or that famous statue
of Balzac by Rodin, my favorite sculptor then.

8

Pressured in confession, Joan gave up my
name. I was threatened with expulsion if
I didn't change my ways. I hitched across
upstate New York to check out other radio
stations, talking music with DJs grateful for
the company, ending up at local coffee houses
where studious looking wallflowers reading
deep books often let me ignite their over-
looked sexual dynamite. Sometimes I got
into fights with local dudes who didn't dig
my intrusions. I kept a coat with blood and
other stains from those adventures for years
as proof of my legendary life. I learned a
lot from the books those girls were reading.

9

At a gig in Bradford, Pennsylvania, a stranger picked up Sam's trumpet. Sam asked him to put it down. The man called Sam prejudiced. Holding out his car keys, Sam said: Take my short for a ride or dance with my date, but put my ax down. Ignoring the keys and the blond, the dark-skinned man raised the trumpet to his lips. Before they touched the mouthpiece Sam made his hands into fists bringing them down hard on the cat's shoulders. I never saw Sam do anything that fast, except spit out notes on his horn. The man dropped like a Marionette whose strings had been cut. Sam snatched his trumpet back, before it touched the ground.

10

Dawn was a local high school senior, caramel complexioned with a smooth round face and cheeks, and big brown eyes. A full grown, darker, Kewpie doll. First time I went to her home, her much darker grandma brought up *KINGSBLOOD ROYAL*, the novel about a white man who discovers he's part black so is therefore legally Negro. When I told her I knew it well, she smiled saying she expected I would. She had decided I was like the man in that book, passing for white. She already knew I read *JET* and *EBONY* and the few books then about Negro history and culture no other white anybody we knew ever did.

11

I interviewed Annie Ross when she came
to Olean with Lambert and Hendricks. Sam
sat behind them with the band that did gigs
with visiting stars, his horn on his lap while
Ross hit notes with her voice only Maynard
Ferguson could reach on a trumpet, Sam's
lip curling like Elvis's snarl, as it did when
he dug something. Ferguson came through
too with his band. I interviewed him as well
asking how he got his extraordinary range. He
claimed: After I wake up I practice for an hour,
eat breakfast, then practice til lunch, after that
I practice til dinner, and if I don't have a gig
to go to, I practice til it's time to go to bed.

12

I learned how to back scratch a record to cue it
up to the next song, then hold it steady while the
song on the other turntable wound down, and
with my free hand leaf through a binder for the
ad copy to read in between. The station higher
ups wanted me to talk more, but my model was
Symphony Sid, whose theme song was sung by
King Pleasure: *Jumping with my boy Sid in the
city… make everything go real crazy over Jersey.*
Now and then I whispered a poem on air mystifying
my bosses or pissing them off. Like one by ex-con
Ray Bremser about the Jersey turnpike: *varoom.*
The one that got me fired was Diane di Prima's
NIGHTMARE 6: Get your cut throat off my knife.

13

I met Angela at the Genesee campus coffee house,
a pretty, dark-eyed, Italian, with a Shirley Mac-
Laine pixie haircut. Later she snuck out of her
dorm, and when she snuck back in it was dawn.
On the way back to Saint Bonnie's my schoolmate
slammed into a snow bank so big everything turned
black, or very dark white. A farmer pulled us out
with his tractor. They confined us to campus but
I ignored that, though I loved my old dorm since
seeing a snapshot of my brother Tommy outside it
in his GI clothes that even in black-and-white you
could tell were olive drab. Angela asked for one
of my poems she published anonymously in her
student literary mag, just before I was expelled.

14

Her name was Carol Lee Fisher, but her
father wanted a boy so they called her Lee,
a high school senior visiting for Press Day.
On my way to escort Pierre Salinger to
where he was to give a speech, I stopped to
flirt with her pretty friend, not noticing Lee
til she cracked wise. I grabbed her program
and wrote a little poem of mine on it, then
told her to read it every night and pass it on
to her kids and have them do the same and
maybe her grandkids would finally compre-
hend it. But instead she found out my name
and wrote to say she loved it. I wrote her
back and asked for a photo she never sends.

This was the poem:

live life
love love

alone
alone
alone

but that was yesterday

love life
live love

together
together
together

this is today

tomorrow?

THE VILLAGE SONNETS

"If you be still and never move, you're gonna dig yourself a well intentioned rut and think you've found a groove."

—Jon Hendricks

1

When Nina Simone played THE VILLAGE GATE I sat on the sidewalk leaning against the grate above the basement stage, sharing a bottle of Gallo half-and-half in a brown paper bag with Destiny and writing poems to send backstage. She never responded. I spied James Baldwin once in OBIES. Cliff said he'd introduce me, but I declined, having heard he was queer. How would I handle a pass if he made one? While Baldwin held court among his admirers, Cliff told me stories about the people in Harlem he sold insurance to, as good as Langston Hughes' *SIMPLE STORIES* only more real.

2

I took my ex-nun sister to see Nina Simone who came onstage in a floor-length dress so tight around her ankles she could take only tiny steps to get to the piano, a Geisha girl walking on ice. I heard rumors about her love life. She was a lesbian, or married to a cop, or having an affair with the guitarist the only white man in her band. I championed the cause of contrast, fixing that sister up on a date with my drummer friend Sblibby. It didn't work out. Maureen was an artist and the coolest white Jersey girl I knew. I fixed her up with Ralphie, my junkie street friend. That turned out to be a mistake too.

3

When platinum-pixie Linda came down from
Olean, I took her to hear 'Trane at the GATE
and to meet Charlie and try to convince them
to be together. She was hurt, as if I were Eddie
telling the runner-up for Miss New Jersey to
climb into the back seat of his customized Ford
and take care of me when I was 15 and she did.
My old man blamed ma's heart attack on my
being kicked out of St. Bonaventure's. So I took
a few courses at Seton Hall but lost interest and
quit after they gave me a weeklong battery of
tests they claimed showed I was smarter than
their faculty. Like winning a million dollars in
Confederate money after The Civil War ended.

4

Princess was a street fixture from the islands.
I never knew which one. I was with her at
OBIES when I first met Cliff, with Mel and
DeWitt. The only empty chairs were at their
table. When we sat down, they started riffing
about how they saw Malcolm speak at
the Harlem mosque earlier that week and
he'd asked Have you kicked a white devil
today? And how little white boys were
polluting the race. When I'd had enough
I stood up and said Which one of you
motherfuckers wants to step outside with
me? They laughed and said Sit down,
we're just fooling with you kid. And I did.

5

Curtis Powell introduced me to my first Greenwich Village pad. I was seventeen, already into the Village scene but as a Jersey interloper digging it from the street. He took me to the crib of an old white cat in his thirties and his dark-haired wife in her twenties, living with a blonde nineteen-year old not only pretty but nice. A pie-slice studio on Cornelia and Sixth Avenue with a big bed and little else to sit on and nowhere else to sleep. It was obvious even before Curtis hipped me to it, they all slept together. I thought I preferred black chicks but if this was beatnik living I wanted some.

6

Curtis was from South Orange, renowned for French kissing a white girl in the public pool in 1957 and smart enough to later earn a scholarship to college and a PhD. Once he took me to a rundown little flat on East 2nd in the building where Ginsberg lived. Bob Kaufman's crib. He wasn't in, just his dark-haired Irish-looking wife Eileen and baby Parker. I read Kaufman's *SECOND APRIL* for free at Figaro's and smoked my first joint after a young black cat invited me to join him for a stroll around the block, continuing our deep discussion begun inside reentering with a whole new perspective.

7

Cliff, Mel, and DeWitt lived on West Third near
the strip joints. Mel reminded me of Jackie
Robinson but with a deeper voice and more
eloquent. He spoke German from when they all
met there in the Army after the war. DeWitt was
the Army's first Negro heavyweight champ. Mel
held the yards gained record for college fullbacks.
Cliff, smaller, thinner and lighter skinned, had
a face freckled like mine. He did so well in the
black market he married the first post-war Miss
Berlin and flew her to the states and a house
on Long Island he paid cash for. When she saw
how race played here, she divorced him and
went on to be the blonde in WHITE RAIN ads.

8

Destiny was one of the gentlest humans I
knew and the first one with no home at all.
One day he jumped out from a doorway to
pull my coat and when I turned around said
Princess is a dyke, she's only using you.
And I said Using me? Someone has found
a use for me? Princess wore men's clothes
that hid a lovely little hourglass figure I
discovered in the bathroom at Mel, Dewitt,
and Cliff's fifth floor walkup where we first
made love. It was one of those tiny ones
with only a toilet and water box overhead
you pulled a chain to flush. They took
baths in the kitchen sink, the deep side.

9

I crashed a Village party with street bros where Red Mitchell was playing with a small combo. When they took a break I stood his bass up and played the melody to *MOANIN'*. Red made it clear he didn't dig strangers playing his ax. I laid it down but drunkenly tripped, putting a tiny crack in it with my pointy-toed boot and was thrown out. For a long time hip Villagers knew me as the little J.D. who kicked a hole in Red Mitchell's bass. At a Brooklyn party Lex Humphries loaned me a rubber when I asked, cause Princess insisted. We went up to the roof, but it was tilted and covered in pebbles that dug into our backs as we almost rolled off.

10

Met Bob Dylan at THE FAT BLACK PUSSY CAT before he recorded or I heard him live, thought he was jive. Passed e. e. cummings in Washington Square only months before he died. He looked like an old man, yet bohemian still in a black beret, a cliché, but not on one from the generation that created it. Diane di Prima and Joel Oppenheimer were friendly. Gregory Corso and LeRoi Jones not. Ginsberg came across like a pushy hustler at times. Kerouac drank way too much, like me. We both got 86'd from THE KETTLE OF FISH. Bob Kaufman, they said, was part European, African, Asian and more, which seemed like the future to me.

11

When Sonny Clark's Trio took a break at THE WHITE WHALE I sauntered to the piano. Pall Mall between fingers still able to play, head drooped toward the keys, a la one of the piano trinity of my iconic history, Bill Evans. I was the only white teenage cat with a black soul I knew. I didn't notice the drummer return til I heard the shhh shhhh shhhhh of his brushes on the snare. Now I really felt solid in my groove. Shit, the cat dug my sound so much he couldn't resist. Then I grinned as the bass joined in. I was the featured act now, the cats backing Clark backing me, making music for all the world to see, especially my new heart's delight: Bambi.

12

The song came to an end. The bassist whispered *HONEYSUCKLE ROSE*, holding up some fingers to indicate the key. But it was beyond me, and the tempo they set was like climbing Mount Everest in shorts and making it to the top before lunch. After a few bars I felt a body sit down beside me on the piano bench. Sonny Clark. He gave me a pathetic look and swung his hip into mine as though knocking me out of the way. Which he was. The band wailed, the audience transfixed as the white kid took a shaky walk back to his table. I always wore shades except when in bed so the tears in my eyes didn't shine in the lights just my obvious flight from the jazz Olympus in my mind.

13

The first place I played piano professionally in Manhattan was on the city's skid row in a joint with a tourist show called SAMMY'S BOWERY FOLLIES where ancient weathered overweight ladies sang like Sophie Tucker, all brass and sass and volume, and dressed like 19th-century dancehall gals in the Hollywood Westerns of my boyhood. There were old men too, vaudeville comics in raggy striped suits and derbies, and white-haired musicians playing piano and banjo. My cousin Rosemary took me there, and another Irish Catholic girl with Mary in her name, and her date, certain I'd pass for eighteen with them in their twenties.

14

Midway through the show this big bosomed old lady looked down at our table and asked who I was, maybe cause I was the youngest in the club. My cousin said Ricky Nelson. Invited to the stage I blushed like crazy as the others insisted I go. Luckily there were no guitars since I didn't play one. I knew the Fats Domino song Nelson covered, so I sat down at the piano to play and sing *I'M WALKIN'* more like Fats than Ricky I hoped, and felt gratified by the applause. The manager, aware I wasn't Nelson, said he'd pay me to be the warm-up act for the main show. I did it for a few months til I discovered progressive jazz.

15

They called her Bambi cause of her big dark Disney-deer eyes that lit up the space around her. We met in OBIES, the bar on Sixth Ave across from West Third where I felt most at home in the world, thanks to a mix of black and white, old and young, straight and queer, beat and hip, junkie and boozer, sophisticated and not, like me, who had no idea OBIES was the name for the off-Broadway theater awards despite the framed posters of winners on the walls like *RED EYE OF LOVE*. I thought Obie was the owner's name. One night there I spied Bambi at a table with other teenagers called colored or Negro. Or spade on the street.

16

After her eyes it was her skin, dark and smooth like coffee without cream, her full lips, nose wide and strong, Indian my spade friends said. Thin as me, a year younger and just graduated from a Catholic girls high school in Atlantic City, I learned after we stop-motion stared at each other before I pulled up a chair. A strange sight to her in my Paul Sargent suit, thin tie, and Ray Charles wide-sided shades, a skinny white boy talking bebop Harlem jive. She and her roommate lived on Tompkins Square, the first black chicks there. We made a date. I arrived with Spanish Harry, who wasn't Spanish, and Mamie, the contrast date I talked him into.

17

Already drunk I got aggressive, Bambi later
said, as we sat on her bed. She was scared til
I fell off onto the floor and she couldn't stop
laughing. Next night I came back to see her
again but an old friend from school had shown
up. She was spending the evening with him,
so gave me a rain check. But I never showed,
exposing her I hoped to how much I was hurt,
then felt like a jerk and called to apologize.
She said she waited for hours. Next time we
met at OBIES where we learned we had even
more in common. Like our fathers: self-made,
grammar-school dropouts with high-school
educated wives. Soon we were a Village item.

18

I was known among friends and family for
falling in love at the drop of an eyelash. But
this time was different. Even Mel, Cliff, and
DeWitt got the intensity of it. We spent every
second we could with each other, getting close
to making love completely then backing off
to save her virginity for the night of our wed-
ding we needed our parents permission for,
too young to marry in Jersey or New York.
In states where we weren't, our so-called
races made it against the law. My father said
Men and women are different, so you start
with one strike against you. If the woman's
not Irish, that's two. Not Catholic, you're out.

19

When my music-man brother Buddy wanted
to marry my Italian sister-in-law, there were
whispered admonitions behind closed doors
about what would be in store for them and
their kids. That sense of forbidden fruit fueled
my boyhood crush on her dark Italian beauty.
My father couldn't argue that we had three
strikes against us: Bambi was Catholic. But
he argued anyway, that our kids would have
it too hard. Out of his hearing, ma said, in
tears, I don't care who you marry if you love
each other but I have to back your father,
he's my husband. Bambi's father hated
white people for what they'd done to him.

20

The night we gave up any hope of marrying
before she turned twenty-one, three long
years away, I decided Fuck them all. Fuck our
families fuck society fuck the stupid racial laws.
Then we finally made love all the way as she
whispered I'm sorry. I asked What for? That I
couldn't wait til we were married. But I swore
before God we were husband and wife. She
always said I was her first lover. Though I had
others, like Princess and Dolores, I felt she was
my first too. Later lying in each other's arms
she said I love you, in a way so surrendered, so
deeply sincere, so much an echo of the feelings
in my heart toward her, I knew it was true.

21

Bambi's roommate didn't dig me so we hung at Mel, Cliff, and Dewitt's talking and making love when they were out. They gave us a key. This was before Cliff got his own place after walking in on Mel having sex with Cliff's lady, the Harlem beauty Theresa. Cliff and Mel were back being friends before long, but Theresa was gone. Cliff's new pad on Thompson had two bedrooms. He rented one to Bull, a married man who used it with just a mattress on the floor for his rendezvous. Bambi and I used it too. There were no examples of happy and accepted mixed-race marriages we knew.

22

Mixed couples were rare, and outside The Village found only in black neighborhoods, where it was always black men with white women. My Jersey friends Teddy and Lynn seemed truly happy, but Lyn worked in an office in Newark where her coworkers were not even aware she was married to a Negro. Her Italian relatives were. And her mother lived with them. My brother-in-law Joe the cop and me were working on the rectory roof one day when Teddy rode by on his Harley. Joe couldn't stop talking about The flying jig on a motorcycle. Teddy treated Joe as he did everyone, with kind acceptance.

23

White people in our parish were upset when
Teddy and Lynn got married in our church,
the first mixed-race wedding there. Except
for parties at their East Orange pad they didn't
socialize much. Just going to the store, people
stared or pointed or made nasty remarks. There
were no movies or books with happy stories
of mixed-race romance, let alone marriage.
Kerouac's short novel about his affair with a
black lady, *THE SUBTERRANEANS*, didn't
end happily. In the movie version she's played
by Leslie Caron. The closest Hollywood
would come to a mixed-race romance was to
turn the black chick into a white French one.

24

THE NEW YORK TIMES ran an article on
teens who copied the Beat or hip style but
came from Jersey or Long Island to The
Village on weekends. DOWNSTAIRS AT
THE DUPLEX had a piano I played when
no one else did. Like the day someone said
There's a reporter at MARIES CRISIS CAFÉ
looking for teenagers who aren't Village
natives. We knew it was us in the story,
the only mixed teenage couple then. The
original Marie was a Gypsy, but now was
a big black lady who played piano and sang.
Her most popular song's refrain was *No-
body cans cans like the garbage man can.*

25

Ted Joans was known as a Beat poet who ex-
ploited the tourist trade, a reputedly hip spade
usually wearing a black beret when I saw him.
In a photo in *THE BEAT SCENE* he sat on the
grass in Washington Square Park with a white
woman and four mixed kids and talked about
Loving every swinging soul. But he gave Bambi
a hard time cause I was white. She was so darkly
beautiful older black men wanted to protect her
or make her their own. Everyone noticed her
lovely face and lithe figure as she danced bare
foot on the grass in the park in flowery summer
dresses, a darker apparition and prediction of
what hippies would be like several years later.

26

Big Brown was a giant of a man, six-
feet-a-lot, with a fierce expression on
his dark face and a way of intimidating
everyone. One day in OBIES he told
Bambi she was wasting her foxy female
self on a skinny little nothing of a sheet,
a gray, a Mister Charlie, just as Cliff
walked in. Before I jumped salty, Cliff
said in his laconic way that if Brown dug
being black so much how come his hair
was gassed? A withering comment about
Brown's conk, a wavy almost Marcel
curl. Brown seemed to cringe, then huffed
and puffed some, before disappearing.

27

In Harlem after visiting a musician friend
on Sugar Hill, me and Bambi following
arcane directions to the subway suddenly
were surrounded by a gang of twenty
or more younger black boys wanting to
know what I was doing with her on their
streets. I said I'm walking with the woman
I love. One of the young dudes who wasn't
the hostile leader, but obviously had in-
fluence, said Aw leave the cat alone. And
they did. More often it was whites giving
us trouble outside the Village. Cursing us
or making threats, or even spitting, like a
sailor did at me in Times Square daylight.

28

The first time we slept with other street kids
in the empty fountain in Washington Square
we woke at dawn and went to the small
water fountain for a drink. I splashed some
on Bambi in fun, but she got all tight-jawed.
When she calmed down, she explained if
her hair, already misshapen from sleeping
on concrete, got wet, it would tighten up
and look even worse. I made sure I never
did that to any black woman again. I wrote
a story about it, adding it to some of the
ones I sent to magazines every week to
always keep some in the mail no matter how
many came back. Like that one kept doing.

29

When the bulls drove through the Washington Square arch, like buses did to turn around til they made Fifth Avenue one way, they'd roust street kids sleeping in the fountain when dry. I'd act all innocent and square when they asked for my I.D. and saw I was from Jersey. Like I was just a teenage tourist looking for Greenwich Village kicks and got caught up with the runaways, the teenage vipers, and juvenile delinquents, as I was called across the Hudson and by some Villagers who knew me. Others would say I was a little Jersey jitterbug or teenage version of what Norman Mailer wrote his famous essay about: *THE WHITE NEGRO.*

30

Cal was Mel's twin but opposite. A high school drop out with a wife and four kids in Pennsylvania. He talked fast with a distinct private accent difficult to understand. Mel enunciated every word like a 19th-century orator. Cal was thinner and darker, with a nose so long and sharply hooked he could pass in profile for an ancient Egyptian. He'd been a paratrooper at fifteen, lying about his age, in post-war Japan then Korea. Mel wore impeccable suits. Cal funky sweatshirts and jeans. Once, walking up the Bowery, on that island where it turns into Third Ave, Cal shouted out to the rainy night: New York, you don't owe me a thing!

31

Sblibby named himself after the black street
term for what Southern racists call *niggery*,
pushing it in everyone's face. Ebony-toned,
my height and weight, but more sinewy and
tight and a few years older, like me he wore
shades indoors and out every waking hour.
I never knew his real name. We met one
rainy afternoon when we were the only ones
at the bar in OBIES. Me at one end, him at
the other with drum sticks and a rubber
practice pad. Yaya let him play along with
the box since we were the only ones there.
When Eric Dolphy blew a phrase making
us both laugh, we recognized each other.

32

Sblibby came into OBIES one afternoon with
a short dark man wearing thick eyeglasses
on his intense angry face. It was Cecil Taylor,
the piano-playing composer innovator changing
jazz. When I extended my hand to slip him
some skin he curled his lip in distaste. Sblib
didn't notice as he raved about me, suggesting
Taylor come to THE WHITE WHALE where
I could display my chops. Surprisingly he did.
There I started in on my version of Ahmad
Jamal's take on *SURREY WITH THE FRINGE
ON TOP*, only even more up-tempo so even
more difficult. But after only a few bars Taylor
got up and walked out without saying a word.

33

In the West Fourth Street station I ran into
Angela and told her about Bambi. She got
upset and wrote me later *You were meant
to marry me, if you marry a colored girl
neither race will accept your kids.* Bambi
quit her job under the influence of Villagers
who promoted free love and life, strangers
to me. Like Chico, light-brown skinned with
thick black hair, usually taken for a Puerto
Rican. He was skinny like Bambi and me,
but quieter than I could be. She wanted us
to hang together. But he had neither a job
nor home so was free to roam the Village
streets with her while I was busy working.

34

When Bambi said Chico was so broke he ate dog
food out of a can cause it was cheaper than Spam,
I ordered her not to see him anymore. She laughed
and went on doing what she wanted. I wanted a
darker version of Dostoevsky's Anna, not a free
spirit. I got so jealous, uptight, and tired of her new
friends and life, when Chico came into OBIES
looking for her, I shoved him against a wall and
spit: I'll rip your lungs out through your throat if
you hurt her. Then drunkenly decided to join the
Army to show them both. My crippled grandma,
who lived with us since Grandpa Dempsey died,
always accused me of cutting off my nose to spite
my face. I never understood what she meant by it.

35

In my usual jazzman's outfit, shades and all,
I went to enlist at the Orange Post Office near
Orange Memorial Hospital where I was born.
An Air Force recruiter leaning against a wall
said What's happenin' man? A hip greeting for
any white man then, let alone one in uniform.
He stuck out his hand, and when I reflexively
did too, slapped mine, an even rarer thing for
a gray dude to do. He said the Army's no place
for a hip cat like you but the Air Force is full
of hip mixed couples. He swore once they saw
me in uniform, Bambi would come running,
our fathers would give in, and I'd be playing
piano in an officer's club in The Big Apple.

36

I signed up for the four-year enlistment. Told
to report to New York the next day I made my
Jersey goodbyes, then met Mel at DOWN-
STAIRS AT THE DUPLEX. Arriving first I
went to the unoccupied piano. After I played
a few tunes the owner said his piano player
quit and offered me the job at a hundred a
month. Cliff paid thirty for his two bedroom
pad. I could support the city life I'd always
fantasized. But too late. When Mel arrived I
told him. He laughed, seeing the humor in it.
I didn't. At OBIES, Cal, Cliff, and DeWitt sent
me off with many toasts, Cliff calling me Mee-
shell, as he always did, adding Bon voyage.

37

For unexplained reasons we were given three more days of freedom. I spent it getting drunk and high with street friends like Andre, a tall dark junkie who knew where to crash. But the last night I ended up alone in a bar unable to stand. When they 86'd me, this square looking Irish chick helped me walk to her crib on East 11th where to my surprise she lived with Pauline a light-skinned mixed teen from Long Island City who ran away at fifteen to arrive in the Village pregnant. Before she began showing, she had a body men fought over. But she was too tough for me. Maybe she had to be. She hooked to get by. Turned out Irish did too.

38

Stumbling in, we woke Pauline up. She threw a clock at us but gave me one twin bed to sleep in and they took the other. I woke at dawn to stare at these two women an arm's length away, Pauline on the outside, Irish against the wall. The covers had slid down and one of Pauline's legs dangled off the side, her slip up past her thighs so everything was showing. I had my horrible hangover, able to focus on nothing but Pauline's everything, feeling oppressed by it, as though it was all I was running from. The power that blossom of female flesh had over me. The Irish Catholic pain and shame and guilt it represented. I split without saying goodbye.

THE SAN ANTONIO/ SOUTHERN ILLINOIS/SAN FRANCISCO SONNETS

"Try to be alive. You will be dead soon enough."

—William Saroyan

1

They fly us to a base outside San Antonio.
The sergeant who meets the plane shoves his
clipboard into my solar plexus as hard as he
can sneering Whose knife YOU runnin' from
PUNK? He's black. The barracks sergeant's
what my spade friends call a Southern pecker-
wood. He has me stand at attention, the backs
of my calves against his footlocker, then he
shoves his finger into my chest til I lose my
balance, falling over backwards, him yelling
I SAID ATTENTION! Doing it over and over
again. When he finally lets me go, a guy eaves-
dropping outside asks me: What'd he do to
you? I punch him in the face. Passing it on.

2

They call me BEBOP cause I can't stop
tapping out beats with my fingers and feet.
Jules is a Puerto Rican from the city, who
shares my love of street history, hipping me
to how overcoats became three-quarter length:
P.R. street gangs had their moms hem them
up, so they don't wrap around their calves to
trip them running from the bulls. Designers
copped it. Murph is a big black dude with
a few teeth missing when he grins. We talk
about how after weeks of marching we
forgot our individual gaits, then spend
hours trying to remember them. We started
with sixty but end with only twenty men.

3

On the plane to Texas a guy calls me a Piney
thinking I'm from the Pine Barrens, Jersey's
Appalachia, cause of my dirty clothes from a
three-day binge, my matted uncut hair and un-
shaved drunkard's chin. They burn my civvies
the first day. My first mail is a card from Mel,
Cliff, and DeWitt, and a letter from Angela who
writes to propose, saying if I refuse her she'll
marry a rich-WASPy-sounding name. Near the
end of basic training they let us go to a dance on
the base. I sit in on a jam that helps get Murph
and Jules and me some dates. Mine is what
my spade friends call redbone, a nurse's aide
whose actual name is Rose, from San Antone.

4

My test scores are so high they offer me
Officers Training School with college grads.
I tell them That jive's for rich white boys, I
was promised I'd be gigging on piano in an
Officer's Club in The Apple. They laugh
and withdraw the offer, sending me instead
to Chanute Air Force Base outside Rantoul,
Illinois, to train as a weather observer, with
more marching, calisthenics, inspections,
and harassment. You can't have toothpaste
residue in the opening, or cap, of the tube,
expecting you to use it every day, then wipe
out the inside of the cap and neck of the tube
with a Q-tip, til they're cleaner than new.

5

One big homely Jewish guy over six feet and
prematurely gray, a teenager too, has huge
ears he wiggles at will. Even at inspections
when the sergeant looks away. They call him
DUMBO. I don't. A sweet gentle giant, he
plants flowers outside the barracks making
the place look happier than it is. Concluding
he's mentally unfit, they kick him out. I
can't wiggle my ears behind the sarge's back
when he shoves his yelling face so close to
mine a kiss seems imminent. I slowly tilt
my head to the side, imperceptibly at first.
The longer the harangue, the more my head
will tilt, until it almost touches my shoulder.

6

I hold the record for article fifteens, they say,
court-martials without courts. They take my
pass and give me extra duty like painting the
latrine. On a Saturday morning while everyone
else sleeps, I get my twenty-five dollar portable
stereo, a small-suitcase-shaped rig that when
opened the turntable swings down and the
sides swing out with speakers, and set it up in
our door-less, stall-less, group bathroom, put
on *GIANT STEPS* and start painting while
scat singing along to it. Guys run in cursing
for being woken up by what they call NOISE!
Blaspheming 'Trane's genius. I take out all
my pent up rage over losing Bambi on them.

7

Though passes are limited to a twenty mile radius, when not restricted to base for some infraction I hitch to Chicago and panhandle enough to grab an unscheduled flight to Idlewild. Twenty-five bucks for a ride in a tin can with seats too close, barely upholstered, service minimal and perfunctory, food often a peanut butter and jelly sandwich. They take off when they have enough folks to make it worthwhile, like flying cabs you share with strangers. I've seen the movie of *PORGY AND BESS* so I get it when I walk into OBIES with the hope of finding Bambi one night and Mel greets me with: Here comes Porgy looking for his Bess.

8

Cal brings his family to Bed Sty where he can afford spacc for his kids and wife Cissie, a big-boned, sweet-faced, dark-brown, country girl who stands her ground in the face of big city intimidations. Lynn and Teddy ask me to be godfather to their first. I take Lois as my date, a tall dark singer in a girl group with a 45: *THE BOY IN THE WATERMELON PINK SHIRT.* KP means peeling potatoes piled high as snow banks in a Jersey blizzard, or washing out garbage cans. You can sing as loud as you want with a hose spraying in metal drowning your voice. I'm singing *CLOUDBURST* when Dick Harvey, a skinny white cat from Maine, joins in.

9

Cats come and go in the service. Scotty, a freckled red-haired tough Brooklyn dude, taller than me, turns up at my barracks to pull me aside, show me his tracks and then whisper: I hear you hit The Apple sometimes, can you score me some horse next time you do? I carry a bag back from Ralphie in my shoe. Scotty snorts a dusting off his finger and declares it soap powder. Ritchie, a good-looking black cat from Bed Sty has his home boys send him gage in the mail. We stroll the parade ground after dark sharing a joint and our taste in music, books, strategies with women, and what we miss about The City.

10

Ritchie and me discover our mutual love for Willard Motley's *KNOCK ON ANY DOOR* when I shout one night *I'm Nick Romano and I WANNA LIVE!* And he answers with the novel's best line: *Live fast, die young, and leave a good looking corpse.* At an R&B show in Danville we push our way close to the stage to get a good look as Mary Wells sings *YOU BEAT ME TO THE PUNCH.* The audience all black except me. I get a lot of hostile looks. More than in Harlem or Bed Sty or Newark. My first taste of Southern black culture. Southern Illinois. I meet a girl who never kissed a white boy but wants to.

11

Willy is long and black. And crazy like
me. We take a bus to Chicago one Friday
and head for South State Street where
an old bum tells me my pants are tight
like a faggot and I oughta get one for some
money. In KING'S PALACE, on North
Clark Street, everyone black or brown, I
dig a young sister really drunk and really
tough. We dance slow and it feels so good.
Then she goes off with her woman. Later I
get a rich 'fay queer to buy us dinner, but
refuse his offer to sleep at his place. Willy
and me get a dollar-a-night room where we
sleep on the narrow bed, without touching.

12

One drunken night I get a tattoo of a spade,
symbolizing my rejection of the white world.
I want it between my pointer and thumb but
since I'm underage the tattoo guy says Not
above the neck or below the wrist. So it can
be hidden under a shirt. He puts it on my right
forearm. When my brother the cop sees it, he
tells our folks I'm in a new gang. When we
get a new sarge, young, my height and freckle
faced, a paddy cat like me but more powerfully
built, rumored to hold the Air Force boxing
title in his weight division, sitting on my foot
locker as he passes, I mutter He don't look
so tough to me. He stops and turns around.

13

When he says Let's see how tough you are
kid, I do what I always did. Bow my head
and charge, fists flying. Usually I pummel
a guy's gut while he batters the back of my
head and shoulders, rarely showing signs of
a fight no matter how badly I'm beat. If he's
been drinking he might even throw up, or quit
before he does. But he grabs my shoulders and
keeps me charging right into a wall. He says Put
up your open hands. Before I even see his fists
move, he's hammering my palms with combi-
nations. In seconds they're swollen. Throwing
an arm around my neck, he says I like you kid,
you got balls, don't give me any trouble. I don't.

14

I get a letter from Bambi saying she's engaged
to Chico and pregnant. I stay up all night going
over it like some hermetic text from the ancients I
have to decipher or die, certain there's something
I'm missing. The next day in a weather class I
keep going over and over it in my head. When the
instructor comes to the back of the room, where
I always sit, and warns me to pay attention, I
get up and withdraw into a far corner, squatting
and mumbling, unaware of what I'm doing. At
the base hospital I lay on a gurney shivering and
talking to myself for hours before a doc gives me
some pills to calm me down and more for later,
then confines me to my barracks for the weekend.

15

The pills to relax me give me energy instead,
make me jumpy to be in the city with friends.
Dolores had asked me to her East Orange High
School prom. I'd turned her down. Now I call
to say I'm coming. Too late, but she'll have her
date drop her in Washington Square after. I get
an unscheduled flight and meet her there in her
prom dress. We spend the night in Cliff's extra
room. Back in Illinois the next Friday I spend
the night in Champaign getting drunk with a
white cat I know. We have to walk miles back
to base, arriving at sunup to find a '54 Chevy
idling outside our barracks. Inside, the owner,
Bucks, is throwing clothes into a duffel bag.

16

Bucks is a big white prepster who heard me
talking to the wind one day and dug it. When
some new guy called me faggy for my tight
civilian pants, I said I dig the way they make
my cock feel man. He backed off. Bucks said
he could see it was just an act. I said I don't
put on any acts, just play music using words
and gestures to create a little melody of mis-
direction to confuse the squares and let them
know there's no reward in fucking with me.
When I ask where he's going Bucks says
he's getting out for good and do I want to
go along. I figure we'll hit The Apple for a
few days, so say Sure. But he heads West.

17

We stop in Rantoul, where two black troops
from East Orange wait on a grand jury, jailed
for stealing a color TV. Dolores has a message
from one of their ribs. I yell it up to a barred
window before being run off. In East Saint Louis
I get Bucks to stop where I know we'll find cool
jazz and hot Sapphires. But the all-black club
unnerves him. Back on the road I sleep through
Kansas, waking for a July snowball fight on the
white-capped Rockies. Later, awed by the desert
night where stars reach down to the horizon,
I wish for someone to share it all with who
might get it, so drop Lee a note as we ride the
high Sierras through Lake Tahoe's rustic charms.

18

In a San Francisco Chinatown hotel, Bucks
sleeps off all his driving alone while I roam
North Beach in my slept-in skinny suit with
action-back jacket and pipe-cleaner pants, my
junkie sky-piece and pointy-toed boots. In
Jimmy Valentine's HOT DOG PALACE where
Columbus and Broadway meet, with only a
quarter left, I eye the jazz-filled box and a slice
of chocolate cake in a glass case, choose the box,
drop my coin in the slot and putting my ear to
the speaker feel a hand on my right shoulder.
Turning to my left as I rise, to avoid getting
suckered, I see Andre from The Apple who
says Got a car? There's a party in Berkeley.

19

I wake Bucks to drive us to BOP CITY, a funky jazz joint where Andre scores, then to a small druggie party in a little white Berkley bungalow where another Michael, a deranged, Jewish, jazz sax player lives with a heartbreakingly crazy young blonde who loves books that she and I deeply discuss after we move in. When he discovers Bucks is from Darien, Andre tells of the wealthy families he knows there. Bucks turns whiter than he already is. Andre had been the only Negro at a Darien private school he says, his English becoming as polished as an old-style movie star's, making mine sound like a spade Bowery Boy's. Later Bucks sells his car for a motorcycle to split for Colorado and the first commune I ever heard of.

20

Crazy Michael gets jealous of me and the blonde so Andre takes me back to North Beach to hang at MISTER OTIS, a jazz club that lets me sit in for free drinks and Andre's lady, a French illegal, hook wealthy johns. She says if I read Herman Hesse's *STEPPENWOLF* it will change my life. It doesn't. Later Andre sneaks the three of us into a hotel across from Valentine's, thanks to the night clerk he knows, then leaves to get me a pint to stop my constant cough from four or more packs of Pall Malls a day, but we know it's to score. She tries to soothe me with sex, but I tell her my preference is for darker chicks. I miss Bambi. When Andre returns with the pint, I empty it.

21

I wake to find a floor littered with sleepers, and an old lady yelling OUT! OUT! Everyone splits except me and Andre. He speaks to the lady like a prince to a peon and she leaves us alone to get dressed. He takes a piss in the sink, does a few ballet turns, then buys me another pint and gets me to call Dolores to propose. I don't know what I'm doing. She says Yes. He disappears. After that I sleep in a half constructed high rise with other vagabonds, like Gaylord, a large queer white cat I know from The Village who wears a blanket with a hole for his head, looking like Jesus or an apostle. Gaylord is the first person I know to give the V sign palm out and say Peace when greeting you.

22

I run into Eileen Kaufman panhandling North Beach tourists with Parker. Like Irish peasant mothers of my Irish grandmother's time wand-'ring the streets of Galway begging with their kids. Paddy O'Sullivan tramps the streets of North Beach dressed like Puss in Boots, wide-brimmed hat with feathery plume, cape, and high fancy boots, declaiming his poems to strangers. We share bottles of booze sitting against the wall outside VESUVIO in the alley next to CITY LIGHTS BOOKS. After a few weeks, my oldest sister Joan wires me fifty to fly back to the base to face a court martial, where I'm fined, busted to no rank, and given thirty days in the stockade.

23

Bucks gets off with a small fine, though he took all his stuff and left a note saying he was *never coming back*. The AP's had to go get him from a Colorado jail. All proof of desertion, which can mean a lifetime in prison. But his mother convinces the general it's all my fault. Once again the rich, or richer, win. At my trial I explain my fiancée is pregnant. Not adding: Not by me and no longer my fiancée. They say Why didn't you ask your Captain for leave? He was on leave himself. Why not your sergeant? He's a white Southerner, my fiancée's black. A sympathetic white Major suspends the stockade, confining me to the barracks I'm already in, with the other fuckups under guard.

24

I short-sheet my bunk so I don't have to make it inspection-ready every day, and sleep in the empty one beneath it. One day I find a tough little muscle-ly blonde guy in my lower bunk. I tell him I sleep there, suggesting he find another empty one. He tells me to go fuck myself and rolls over. I raise my right combat boot and bring it down on his head. He jumps up as if on fire and finds another. When a big new white country boy spies Dolores's photo over my locker he says I see we got a nigger in here. I point the sharp end of my pocket nail file at him and say That's my wife, use that word around me again I'll take out one of your eyes before you can kill me. He never says it again.

25

When my training is done, to teach me a lesson they assign me to the only state not integrated an iota, South Carolina. But first I take leave to The Apple where Dolores has moved. Jersey hip, short, dark, and tough, she's what the old folks call homely. But I dug her from in front, cause she accepts me as I am. Only I love Bambi, not her. So, I start an argument over how many kids we should have, to get out of my drunken proposal, and do. In a new bar on Bleecker Cliff takes me to, I run into two street kids who everyone calls Joe The Puerto Rican, and Girl. They call me Bambi's Old Man.

26

When I get mad at being linked with Bambi, Joe The Puerto Rican tells me she's in a little crib on East 14th fucked up and alone, being taken advantage of. He'll take me there if I want to do the same. I pretend I do. He leads me to her pad at the top of chicken shit encrusted stairs and points to her door with a nasty grin from a few steps down. I kick him as hard as I can. He lands at the bottom of the stairs screaming YOU CRAZY MOTHER-FUCKER! But when I beckon with my hands for him to come back up, he runs. I'm always making threats I doubt I'd ever keep, but in the moment mean. This is the just opposite.

27

I open the door to an unlit room, hear some-
one breathing deeply in the dark and know
it's her by the perfume of her presence I can
never forget and haven't yet. The room so small
I could stretch my arms and touch both walls.
The only furniture a cot-size bed she's asleep
in. Lying down beside her, the heat from her
fever burns. Her eyes open. I say It's me. She
says I know, don't fuck me I'm sick. I tell her
No no no no no baby, I'm not here to fuck you,
I'm here to take care of you. She gets as close
to crying as I ever saw her, or her me, then
whispers I just don't want you to get it too. I
whisper, God how I still love you. And I do.

28

As sunlight begins to seep in through the
dirty token window revealing cigarette
burns on her still soft skin, I want to find
the men who put them there. Before she
wakes there's a banging on the door. I
open it to a short stocky old white bald
guy in a cheap suit demanding rent for the
room. My rage backs him down the stairs
as he yells about calling the cops. Helping
her into the one dress she has left, I take
her to Mel and DeWitt's since Bull is at
Cliff's. DeWitt lets us sleep in his room,
he takes the couch, while for days I bathe
her and nurse her and hold her all night.

29

Bambi says she and Chico crashed at various pads with other street kids who introduced them to cough syrup and speed. The drugs turned him mean, so as he dozed on his stomach, shirt off, in the heat of a summer day, she sat down beside him and slowly traced circles on his back with a razor blade. He awoke to a wet sensation, touched himself back there and screamed at the blood on his fingers. She knew superficial razor cuts can cause a lot of blood but no real harm, though the scar will last. After that, Chico's dad came down to the city to drag him back to the upstate farm it turns out he came from. It also turned out his family was Greek, and his name wasn't Chico.

30

The first time I get Bambi to smile again it makes my heart dance. When she finally laughs, it feels like I've just been born and everything is new. Despite all she's been through, she still speaks calmly, with perfect diction, and carries herself regally. When she grows strong enough we venture out to Washington Square where we sit on a bench reliving what seems so long ago when we first fell in love. Then she tells me she's pregnant by a man she doesn't intend to tell. Abortions are illegal and risky especially for someone like her who can't afford to fly to a Caribbean island for a safe and legal one.

31

Bambi swears she'll never return to the
dire conditions I found her in or lose
control of her life again. She never will,
like that. We sit on that bench talking
all day and decide she'll go to her folks
til the baby comes, then give it to foster
care while we get back together. If that
works out we'll marry and get the baby
back. Suddenly out of the gathering dark
there's Ralphie returning my five from
the jive heroin deal, insisting on buying
us dinner at a new diner on Sixth Ave,
and after, buying me a pack of Pall Malls
and Bambi some glossy woman's mag.

32

After Bambi gets on a bus to AC, I get so drunk
Spanish Harry has to drive to the city, carry me
to his car with Dewitt's help, and drive me back
to Jersey where my old man and brother-in-law
are leaving for Florida. I come to, lying on the
back seat asking Joe to pull over so I can puke. I
spend the day doing that, my father wanting to
find a hospital. We talk him out of it. Stopping
early at a motel I get some pancakes down and a
solid night's sleep. Next morning they drop me
at the front gate of Donaldson Air Force Base
outside Greenville, South Carolina, and drive on
to Hialeah. I'm in my dress blues but wearing my
shades the guard makes me remove before entering.

THE SOUTH CAROLINA /ATLANTIC CITY SONNETS

"But to look back from the stony plain along the road which led one to that place is not at all the same thing as walking on the road; the perspective to say the very least, changes only with the journey; only when the road has, all abruptly and treacherously, and with an absoluteness that permits no argument, turned or dropped or risen is one able to see all that one could not have seen from any other place."

—James Baldwin

1

Tom Mosley left St. Bonaventure's to return home to Greenville, so I get on a bus outside the base and tell the white driver to let me know when he gets to Tom's street. He says That's Niggertown you don't wanna go there. I say Yeah man I do. Then bop back to my favorite seat, the last. The bus doesn't move. Pointing to a sign up front, the driver asks if I see it. I can't read it from that far through my shades so say No. He reads loudly *COLORED MUST SEAT FROM REAR*. He says that means I have to move up front. I say I dig where I am man. An old white lady yells Get the sheriff. An elderly, gaunt, sad-eyed, dark gentleman sitting near me says Please cap'n, we don't need no trouble. I get up and get off the bus.

2

When I make it to Tom's, his mom explains Negroes aren't allowed in restaurants, or the public pool, or the movie theater. They even aren't allowed at the drive-in movie in their own cars. Tom's father owns a used car lot. Tom has a little red sports car he drives us to THE GHANA in. Billed as *THE WORLD'S LARGEST COLORED RESORT*, it has a motel, pool, golf course, picnic grove, and a nightclub featuring the best acts on The Chitlin Circuit. They don't want to let me in, but Tom talks the door man into admitting me as a black music act's manager. They have a tiny bar off the main room, with a view of the stage, just for them.

3

The base is federal property, so legally integrated. But the mess hall's voluntarily segregated, the dances officially so. At the black dance my first time, when stopped at the door, I lie that my great grandma was part Negro. Most girls there don't want to dance with me, but Booty Gal does. That's the name her boyfriend Roberts gave her and she digs cause she's so skinny like me she has no booty at all. He's a really smart man who out of uniform dresses like a vaudeville dandy: striped suit, two-toned shoes, black derby, and gold-handled cane, and accepts me as I am without question.

4

Tom stays away from clubs like THE HOLE as local hip spades call THE FLAMINGO. I discover it one night wandering downtown with its *COLORED* and *WHITE ONLY* signs. The black section doesn't need signs. Through an open door comes live R&B, funkier than up North. I follow it down a worn old stairway to a basement door where a big bulky man stands behind a table with weapons taken from patted-down patrons. When he says This is a colored club, I do a version of what I always do: I lie. I tell him my grandma was Italian when South Carolina's laws said Italians were non-white, so that makes me legally colored.

5

The big bouncer gets an older man with a thin mustache in a conservative suit, who says if the sheriff comes round he'll close them down when he sees me. I tell him I'll explain to The Man about my ancestry. He gives in but says I have to sit at the darkest end of the bar and not mingle. After digging the trio on the tiny bandstand, and a few shots backed by beer, I go to drop a tear, as my father would say, but forget to lock the door of the broken-down broom closet of a bathroom, just big enough for a toilet and tiny dirty sink. I hear the door open behind me and the music grow louder then diminish, then a hook snap into an eye.

6

I zip up, turn and try to squeeze by a short dark wiry guy with a skinny brim over a doo-rag hanging out beneath. The uniform of a bad dude, a thug, a gangster, and I know it, even before I see the knife flash. He pushes the blade against my neck. Whatchu want cracker? Lookin' for slaves motherfucker? You just loves you some black folks Mister Charlie? I say, I'm scopin' out Sapphire and diggin' the sounds, as far as spades and grays go, seems to me there's as many asshole spooks as asshole peckerwoods bro. After a long silent beat he laughs, snaps his knife shut and it's in his pocket before I realize I'm holding my breath, and let it out.

7

As we slap skin he says I'm Dusty and you
alright, anybody give you shit you get me, I'll
cut the motherfucker, nobody fuck wif Dusty.
Back at the bar I notice a pretty little woman
with short straightened pixie hair, a darker and
curvier Jean Seberg wearing shades. Catching
each other's dark lenses, she near the dance
floor, me at the shadowy end of the bar in this
segregated catacomb, I get up and she moves
into my arms for a slow dance. THE HOLE's
first mixed couple, they say. When the song
ends we don't notice. The mustache man
does. On our way to Nickletown, as black
folks call it, I learn her name is Della Jones.

8

Della says she'll soon be going to Connecticut,
recruited by a company promising Southern
black teenage girls a better high school education
if they take jobs as servants in white homes up
North. Hard work, but she'll be away from legal
segregation, which is all she wants. We cut
across the park, recently closed to prevent acci-
dental integration, the road through it still used.
Out of matches I wave at passing cars for a light.
She voices fear of us being caught together by
the wrong people. A car full of black cats brakes
and they tell us to get in. One asks me something
in Spanish and I mumble some Spanish back.
He says, I told you my man's a Puerto Rican.

9

Dropped off on the other side of the park,
Della says that I can go no further. We step
into the shadows near a low brick building
to kiss, and keep kissing. A school she says.
I break a small pane of glass in the locked
door with my jazzman-suit-jacketed elbow
and take her hand to wander dark silent halls
peering into rooms with tiny desks and chairs
til we find a place with enough space to
make love in, again and again, on a small
pile of our clothes on the little gym floor,
naked in each other's arms, not letting go,
not even when we hear the low hum of a
motor as a search light sweeps the windows.

10

We keep the rhythm of our contact alive in
a way that slows but never stops, waiting to
be discovered. I whisper They'll have to
carry us out like this. But their searchlight
doesn't shine down to where we are on the
floor, and they don't get out of their car,
just drive away. We celebrate with more
rhythm, falling asleep exhausted, still inter-
twined. When daylight begins its slow glow,
I wake, inside her still, to kiss her fine dark
face. Her eyes open. Seeing the light she
lets out a small sound of fright, insisting we
have to leave immediately, and separately
so no one up that early sees us together.

11

It's hard to find places to make love, but we
do one moonlit night on the hard clay ground
behind the little gospel church in Nickletown.
The day before she leaves for Connecticut I run
into Della outside the record shop downtown
and take her hand. As white people glare, she
leaves it there. Two nights before she split, I
integrated a mess hall table with a lone black man
reading and asked what it was. He showed me
ATLAS SHRUGGED. We started an extended riff
about all we believe that lasted til dawn, and on
and off ever since. Gene knew who I was cause
he'd met a fine dark little lady named Della, who
told him about a crazy Jersey paddy-cat flyboy.

12

I work alone in a tower at the end of the run-
way reporting weather conditions, or in an
office making weather maps. Gene joins me
on my graveyard shifts sometimes. A tall
handsome soft-spoken cocoa-toned man with
big black framed glasses, I thought he intro-
duced me to the thrill of lying on top of the
metal shack at the end of the runway in the
middle of the night, high, watching giant cargo
jets take off and land, so close overhead you
feel you can reach out your hand and touch
the screaming mass of metal as it takes what
seems like forever to pass over you, leaving
your heart racing. But he says it wasn't him.

13

First time I call Bambi from the barracks pay phone, she's in her bathtub in AC and happy to be after living on the streets or that 14th Street crib. I picture the bathtub scene in *THE SEVEN YEAR ITCH*, but with Dorothy Dandridge not Marilyn Monroe. Though Bambi's more darkly regal, beautiful, and soulful than either. On the graveyard shift that night, huge transport planes descend on the runway in the dark. Out of them march soldiers twice the size of anyone in my outfit, wearing head gear I've never seen before like red berets. A few days later we all huddle round the radio at work listening to JFK give an ominous speech about Russian missiles in Cuba.

14

More strange fighting troops come and go to a staging area in the Florida Keys where they camp in tents like Boy Scouts at a jamboree, as I'm told when I find out I might join them. One night I wake to knocking on the cubicle door across from mine. Told the next day a barracks mate is on his way to the Florida embarkation camp, I ask Why? Sarge says the man is part of the first wave of the invasion. But the guy, an office clerk, can hardly handle a rifle. Sarge explains that the guy is one of our expendables. They fill the percentage of troops expected to die in the first wave, with ones they can spare.

15

They need a mobile weather unit as soon as
troops land, to send back weather stats for
bombing runs. We practice setting up field
instruments as guys from our barracks dis-
appear night after night. I know how to use
an M1 rifle and proved it on the firing range.
But I hate guns. My brother, brother-in-law,
and other cops in our clan keep theirs hidden
when not on duty or guarding my old man at
Essex County Democratic Party meetings. I
never had the urge to find them or touch them
or use them. Even empty. Even as a teenager.
When Khrushchev backs down we're told
to keep our mouths shut about it all. And do.

16

I still have nightmares from newsreel footage
when I was a kid of emaciated bodies bull-
dozed into pits, or flicks about returning vets
gone psycho killing innocents, or rumors of
what older boys experienced in the war, like
how the Krauts or Japs got GI prisoners
naked, paraded nude women before them
til they were erect, then inserted thin glass
tubes up their urethras and hit them with
hammers. And we believed it. Just like we
believed the stories about lampshades made
from human skin and soap from human fat
and all the ugly war stories we whispered
about. The vets just kept their mouths shut.

17

Gene is from the Midwest, his crew from
all over, even deeper South. All smart and
smarting under segregation. Thanks to him
they accept me. I get to ride around in the
old gray '49 Chevy they share, with a sign
one of them made under the shotgun seat
visor: *WHITES SEAT FROM REAR.* Asked
to drive in the even more racist countryside,
I find out why when stopped by a sheriff's
deputy who says Where you goin' son wid
alleez nigras in your car. In my best South-
ern accent I tell him they've been helping
fix my daddy's barn and I'm taking them
back to where they belong. He waves us on.

18

Doc Gandy, a dark middle-aged, and at times
effeminate man not much more than boy sized
owns THE GHANA, with an apartment over
the club, a house in town, and office for seeing
patients. Rumor has it he controls the black
drug trade in the area, giving him more power
over some of the entertainers who play his club.
The first time I'm there without Tom, from the
small, white-managers room I dig a big band
with a gaggle of female dancers, BABY JUNE
AND THE SWINGING SHEPHERDS. When
they take five, I compliment June, a handsome
baby-faced elegant young man, on his band
and troupe and ask to meet one of the dancers.

19

June jumps salty at my interest in the fox of
his show, but when he gets I'm just a musician
who digs fine women, he invites me to jam after
the club closes, then digs my playing enough to
ask me to join their run at THE GHANA, since
he has no piano player and there's a piano on
stage. He supplies what looks like a fancy
waiter's uniform with a bright red cummerbund,
and leads us into the club each night, bursting
through the door, shouting as we run to our spots
onstage to start dancing and playing, June on
trumpet and vocals, others on brass, reeds, bass,
and drums, and one crazy paddy cat pounding
the keys while standing up, Little Richard style.

20

June likes it when I whip my head around
to make my hair swing like Cab Calloway.
The black-only audience goes wild. Doc Gandy
wants to see me after my first show so sends a
couple of his young muscle dudes to bring me
upstairs where he lounges on a big bed like a
smaller, darker, male Miss Scarlett and quizzes
me on why I want to be with colored folks. I
say I love good music and foxy women and
don't like anyone telling me where I can't or
can go to dig or blow that music or meet those
women, colored or not. He seems to get a kick
out of it and lets me play behind acts with no
piano player after June's troupe is long gone.

21

I meet, and sometimes back, musicians and singers well known on The Chitlin Circuit, and beyond. Like B. L. who has a new R&B hit. After her gig, she asks me to join her for a late dinner where she pats the chair next to her and when I sit down reaches under the table to squeeze my johnson so hard I'm not only startled but have tears in my eyes. After letting go with a big smile, she invites me to her room later. I go, but not without a little trepidation and a lot of fortification. When I get there, her entourage surrounds the bed she's sitting up in, so all we do is talk. She signs a wallet photo for me as a keepsake.

22

Marty is the hippest white cat I meet in South Carolina, a Jewish jazz sax player my age from Baltimore. The way he dresses when out of uniform is so casually cool I try to emulate it. He's so laid back it seems like he lives in another state than we all do. One Friday Gene and me use the Chevy for his first trip to New York. He remembers Marty coming too. I don't. Unless we dropped him in Baltimore, where I recall old black ladies early Saturday morning scrubbing three-step marble stoops on funky old row houses. Arriving in The Apple we head for O-BIES, where Cliff picks up the conversation of months before like I'd taken a bathroom break.

23

On another weekend, Gene and me take the old Chevy to legally segregated Atlanta to try and meet coeds at Spelman. I drunkenly try to get us a room in a cheap hotel, but when they see Gene they refuse to let us in. I curse them out til Gene pulls me away to sleep in the car. At dawn we integrate an empty diner. The old white cook doesn't want to serve us, but his old white waitress doesn't want the hassle she can see I might cause, so she talks him into it since we're the only customers anyway. By the time we finish our eggs and grits, other customers arrive, glaring at Gene and me as we split.

24

One weekend night I go with Gene's crew to Anderson and the home of a very tall black queer living with an old lady I assume is his grandma. She hates 'fays so me and LJ, who some folks call high yellow, have to avoid the kitchen where she spends her time cooking, drinking, and badmouthing crackers. The first time she met LJ she threatened to throw a pot at him for being The Man. It's hard for him to live that down, or his having to hang with me behind closed doors so she never sees our light-toned skin. Eventually she passes out, then LJ and me are free.

25

On the way we stop for food, booze, and women. I go in with Roberts for Booty Gal who lives in a shack beneath a water tank at the bottom of a rain gully with her little girl and sister's family. I don't go in when we stop for Big John's rib. Last time we picked her up I did, but her father came home drunk to find a white devil in his house, got his pistol and shot at me as I ran out the door with the rest of the fellas. He missed. After that I got myself a one-shot little derringer, but I could never remember if the safety was on or off. Feeling for it in my pocket made me worry I'd blow my johnson off by accident. So I got rid of it.

26

When our towering host saw me, he made a phone call to say I got what you always wanted sister: W, H, I, T, E. When she shows up everyone thinks she's the homeliest thing they've ever seen. Tall with ashy black skinny legs and a long horse face. But I dig her and never think about why or why not. Everyone calls her Big Alice. We share a bed-room with Big John and Sonia. Our host hanging around to catch us all undressing. I strip to my G.I. boxers, waiting for him to leave. When Big John removes his jockey shorts, our looming host makes a joke about why they call him that, then leaves us alone. Alice has no qualms getting naked in front of us all. Sonia keeps her bra and panties on.

27

Younger than me, Alice seems older and tougher yet kisses so tenderly, holding my head between her big hands. Across the room Sonia moans, Big John curses softly. No sound from Alice, and little movement above her waist though nonstop below. Her lips more voluptuous than any I've known, we never stop kissing til morning, and dancing with our hips. Our host, up too late to catch us dressing, asks her How was my surprise? Alice, who hasn't said a word since coming thru the door the night before, says Jus' like a nigga. Ain't this girl a bitch? He says. When I tell Gene he says The big problem in the 'sixties is going to be getting black people to accept white people.

28

Called in by the base doc for a syphilis test, it comes back negative. I'm the only white guy on the list. The others are Roberts and the cats in Gene's crew, exposed to it some-how and among those blamed is Big Alice. Roberts takes it in stride, so I try to too. A young white dude, Willy Dorton, finds me at the piano in the music room and picks up a guitar to play along. Shorter than me, with wavy auburn hair, a friendly smile on a boyish face, and slow Southern style of speaking and moving, he wants us to start a band. I need the extra bread. The court martial left my pay at barely fifty a month.

29

We play rockabilly til I can't take it anymore.
In the middle of a gig I walk off the stand and
out the door. Willy follows. I tell him I'm goin'
where you can't. When I close THE HOLE
craving more booze, he's waiting to take me
to THE DIXIE HOTEL, the name of an old
Jersey-shore Victorian my Uncle Lydie and
Aunt Peggy spent their honeymoon at, and me
at fifteen my first all night with a girl, eighteen.
Willy leads me up a flight of stairs to a lobby
with a bar, chairs, and white cats in jeans and
white tees, sleeves rolled, playing poker. They
belong to the Harleys out front. A tough-talking
old white lady sends two chicks to sit on our laps.

30

With their ponytails and jeans, the hookers look
like high school seniors, cute in a country way.
Willy takes his to a room while mine grows
tired of my lack of interest in anything but
drinking. The leader of the bikers, a tattooed
cat with early Elvis hair and jailhouse muscles
eyes me with a sarcastic smile, as he asks if I
want to play, making it clear I have no choice.
Then even clearer he's cheating. I lose all my
money and try to quit, but the biker says I can
owe the pot and get it later from my friend.
After I lose another ten he says Get the money,
now. I knock on the door Willy disappeared
behind. He yells Come back later. No, I say.

31

Willy opens the door pulling up his pants, the girl on the bed behind him. I ask him for ten. He says he gave the hooker all he had. The biker empties Willy's pockets. Nothing. He throws me against the wall and turns my pockets out too: nothing there either. Before the biker rearranges my face, Willy yanks my twenty-five dollar high school ring off my finger and gives it to him. Stumbling out into the early light Willy says he asked the hooker to marry him. She wouldn't say til she had all his money, then said No. Two cops pull up to us. The one riding shotgun asks Where y'all comin' from? He smiles when Willy tells him. I say The Dixie's a jive front for lowlifes.

32

The cop wants my I.D. When I open my wallet he sees the photo of Bambi. Who's that? The rib I'm gonna have freckle faced li'l spades with. Where you from boy? The Apple. He turns to Willy to translate. New York. He asks Willy, Where you from son? Kingsport Tennessee. You best explain to your Yankee friend we don't go for no nigger love round here. Willy says: I'm gone be best man at his wedding. The cops drive us to the city line and tell us to stay out of Greenville. On the long walk to the base I pick up every rock, bottle, or piece of debris I stumble over and throw it at anything breakable, like gas station windows with their *COLORED* and *WHITE ONLY* signs for restrooms.

33

I'm in a blackout when I throw the last rock through a latrine window in my barracks yelling FUCK SOUTH CAROLINA! Luckily no one's in it. Sarge makes me pay with extra duty. Next day the paper has a story about a gang of teenage vandals *wreaking havoc for miles* along the highway. Willy keeps pushing me to take him to THE GHANA, so I do. After a few drinks in the white managers side bar, he snaps to, like he's been whacked in the head, turns to me, eyes shining, and declares Man there's a lot of beautiful women here. He's only noticed white women before, but now can see the beauty in many of the black women in the crowded club.

34

Willy borrows my red corduroy vest one night returning it next day covered in dried blood. He'd been taken to the hospital after the cops broke up a bar fight where he was badly beaten by several crackers. One slashed Willy's face with a hawk, as hip spades call those curved knives we cut linoleum with, for his insistence on the beauty of colored chicks. He took it right into the lion's den cause it's familiar to him and he naively believed, as I sometimes do too, that anyone will feel the way we do if they have the opportunity. But it's just me, then him, anywhere we go in the segregated South.

35

I'm in THE HOLE when a cat from the base, shorter than me but hard and explosive, wants to know what the fuck I'm doing in a black club when he isn't allowed in white ones. I say Just cause I ain't scared to go where I want ain't my fault if you are. He punches me, knocking me to the floor. An older black man, who knows me the way bar flies know each other, helps me stand and whispers If you got to go down, go down fightin' my man. But instead of a fight, the tough little black dude says Meet me outside tomorrow night and we'll see who's afraid, peckerwood. When I tell Dusty, he insists I need to get myself another piece.

36

We drive far out in the country to a small shack. A woman answers the door in a little slip type thing. She has brown flawless skin, long black hair and a face more perfect than I've ever seen. Dusty asks for her old man. But he isn't there. I just stare. Dusty asks if she has any booze. We drink, while she stares back at me like I'm staring at her, till Dusty says I'm gone cop some zees in the 'sheen. As he goes to the car, she takes my hand, leading me to one of those old iron beds I've only seen in movies, where we begin to make love, like a fantasy I never knew I had, that turns surreal when I realize near the bed is a crib with a baby asleep in it.

37

A framed photo on a beat up old dresser of a young black man in a Navy uniform makes me feel guilty, doesn't stop me. Moving on top she whispers You the most beautiful man I ever seen. Overwhelming firsts: a woman on top, and being called beautiful. When I was younger my old man had what seemed a huge mirror hung in our living room to make the little area appear bigger. When I came downstairs to go out, there was my image a few feet across the small space. I'd check my hair. If my father was in his armchair reading the paper while listening to his favorite radio station play sappy string versions of once popular tunes, he'd say Vanity have I ever offended thee. Sounding like the indictment it was.

38

I say No it's you who's beautiful. She doesn't respond, intent on her sensual moves I pray will go on forever, but we reach the end together. While I dress she goes to the little kitchen and cooks up some eggs. As I eat, neither of us saying a word, she leans against my shoulder playing with my hair, now and then kissing my neck. Like being in a secret movie of the heart's most amazing mysteries. Back in the car I wake Dusty. He doesn't ask about my night, just says the cat with the guns isn't the father of the baby, that cat's gone. He says he should go to THE HOLE with me. I say No it's cool. Pretending I believe it.

39

An old Olds pulls up to THE HOLE with the tough little cat and four other rough looking young black dudes I don't know. He motions for me to slide in beside him and the driver. I'm glad to be next to the door as we head for the countryside. Nobody saying anything. We are all aware young black men like them are being killed in the South what seems like every day for stuff a lot less provocative than integrating a white bar. Eventually the tough little dude says This one. The driver pulls into a half-empty patch of gravel outside a rundown obviously redneck bar. Then we get out and slowly walk into the place.

40

There are two old white guys at the end of the bar and a few couples at tables. The black cats freeze as the occupants glare, but when I walk to the bar, they follow. I sit on a stool across from the old bartender and order a shot of J. W. Dant. He just stares. Turning to the guys standing behind me I ask What'll you all have? They're staring back at the bartender, not saying anything until the tough little cat says A beer. The white guys at the end of the bar mumble shit I can't hear. The bartender looks mad. These boys with you? I get what cover he's looking for. Yep. He sees his out and takes it: One drink that's all.

41

As the black cats empty their glasses and put them on the bar, the barman picks each up and smashes it on the floor. The little guy ready to explode, doesn't. As we split I shout Y'ALL KNOW WHAT JUST WENT DOWN, THIS JOINT'S BEEN INTEGRATED! Then leap through the door as two men run after me. I make it into the front seat as a gunshot echoes. The driver peels out. Total silence til it's clear we aren't being followed. As if on cue everyone bursts out laughing, hooting and slapping each other's hands, including mine before anyone remembers I'm the only white, or to me the lightest, cat in the car.

42

Gene gets his crew to join us at the base movie theater for *WEST SIDE STORY*. As it starts and the actors playing New York City gang members begin to sing and dance, most of the white men in the audience jeer and howl at the screen, mocking all that sissy stuff. I dig the Broadway album: the romantic honesty in the lyrics, the jazz influence in the music, and see the plight of Bambi and me in Maria and Tony, so I stand up and yell IT'S A FUCKIN' MUSICAL! IF YOU DON'T LIKE SINGIN' 'N' DANCIN' THEN FUCKIN' LEAVE! No one does. But they all stay real quiet for the rest of the film. Probably cause Gene's crew is there with me.

43

Bambi doesn't want to wait to get married, so she talks her pastor into marrying us by not telling him I'm white. I buy her an engagement ring on the installment plan from a catalog and call my ma. She gives the phone to my old man. I tell him Bambi's pregnant by another man but I love her and believe marrying her is the right thing to do. We argue til in frustration he yells into the phone You're no longer my son nor part of this family, I never want to see or talk to you again! Then hangs up. I just stand there alone in the phone booth, one of those metal and glass jobs that look like the future compared to the old wooden one they still have in OBIES.

44

When my siblings are told of my engagement, my brother the friar writes from Japan advising *Be prudent because of the racial tensions in the United States at present.* My brother the music teacher writes that *Love doesn't last, at least the first glow, then being married is just like living with anyone else.* Adding *All women are crazy, no exceptions.* My sisters are okay, but Joan writes that our brother the cop is *thinking of quitting the force and moving*, telling her if I *marry a colored girl I'll never be allowed in his home or near his kids again.* But the wedding is scheduled and the banns read out in Bambi's church on the three Sundays before it.

45

Before I hitch to AC for the wedding, ma
calls to say: Daddy's sorry and can't sleep he
feels so bad, he's driving down to meet you at
a motel outside Winston Salem. My first ride
is with a white truck driver older than me,
who asks Where y'all headin'? When I say
Atlantic City he asks What for? I say To get
married. He inquires about my bride. I tell
him She's beautiful and black. He gets quiet.
I wait to be kicked out of his truck. He finally
says Pretty gutsy marryin' a colored girl con-
siderin' all the shit y'all gone git. Then he
wants to know how Jersey coloreds compare
to the Southern coloreds he knows personally.

46

The trucker invites me to join him for supper in
a white restaurant-bar where we meet two chicks.
After some drinks, me and one of the girls begin
slow dancing to the jukebox, closely and sensually.
The manager tells us Quit it, this is a family place.
The girl leads me to her car in the dark where we
make it in the back seat. She is, as I write in a
journal, *beautiful and plain and ordinarily lonely*
like all of us. She wears glasses and seems bright,
and rips through the back of my dress blue shirt
with her nails, drawing blood. Afterward she tells
me, in her heavy South Carolina accent, she's
nineteen but already divorced. When the trucker
and me split she wishes me luck with my marriage.

47

The trucker takes me as far as he's going, then two young women pick me up on the side of the highway. By now it's raining. They tell me they're both divorced and think I'm cute, but all I want to do is sleep in their back seat. It takes two more rides to where my old man is waiting. When I enter his motel room he's asleep. I undress in the dark, stuff the ripped shirt with its blood stains in my duffel bag and get into the empty twin bed as quietly as I can. But as soon as I do, he asks if I'm alright, not mentioning what he said about me no longer being his son or part of the family. Over breakfast he asks about my bloody shirt.

48

On the ride to Hyattsville, Maryland, where my brother Buddy the music man lives, my father says he'll drive me all the way to Jersey if I give up marrying Bambi. After hours of arguing, he drops me at Buddy's. My grammar school drop-out old man taught us to treat everyone the same and has Negro pals and would never let anyone use the N-word around him when we were growing up. When he gets home he sends me one of the only letters he's ever written, about how difficult it'll be for any kids we have, and asks for some sympathy for what he calls: *Us unintellectuals.* And for white people slow to acknowledge that changes need to be made in the way colored people are treated.

49

I make it to AC and find a cheap little hotel run by tough-looking Italians a few blocks from the boardwalk, almost empty in the off season. Bambi's house is bigger than my family's, though she's an only child. Her father's at his dry cleaning business. Her attractive mother, hair pulled back a la Billie Holiday, wants me to understand how grateful she is for my marrying her daughter, knowing I'm not the father. She assures me Bambi will never do that again. Away from the house, Bambi and I kiss, her growing belly between us. She says her mother and aunt are trying to set up a meeting between her father and me but are, so far, unsuccessful.

50

When I tell Bambi where I'm staying, she says They'll never let me in there. But she has a friend whose parents died in a car accident, their house is where their crowd hangs out or crashes. But the door to the room we grab doesn't lock and others keep barging in. So I take her to see *WEST SIDE STORY*. As we exit the theater, the white folks stare at this very pregnant teenage black girl and very white young man holding hands. Bambi is upset about Tony's death and doesn't get why I'd want her to see that, since we both see me as the Tony in our love affair. She dismisses the rest as Hollywood fluff compared to the real life stuff she's struggling through.

51

Walking past a funky black motel, Bambi wants
to get a room. Scared some bad dudes might roll
me, or her father find out and want to shoot me,
more than he already does, I suggest we go to
her friend's. She insists on the motel. Thinking
I'm afraid cause I'm white, she says The desk
clerk will assume I'm a hooker and you're my
john. I get upset that she thinks our love could be
seen that way. She walks away in a huff. I have
to catch up to tell her how much I want to make
love but just don't want to fuck things up. Next
day her father agrees to meet. I arrive early in
my dress blues, her aunt and mom in their Sunday
best, so he'll have more respect for our meeting.

52

Bambi's father is a small but tough-looking
very dark-skinned man, eyes raging as his sister
introduces us, then leaves us with a bottle and
two glasses. I expect him to pull out his piece,
so feigning the bravado of the streets I ignore
the glasses, reach for the bottle, drink from it,
then hold it out to him. He looks surprised but
takes a swig and hands it back to see if I'll wipe
the mouth. I take another slug and return it. We
don't say a word as we finish it off. He calls
for another and this time takes the first swig
and passes it to me, asking why I want to marry
his daughter. Do I know it isn't my kid? I say
I do but I love her, so it doesn't matter to me.

53

We take our time with the second bottle. He tells me why he hates white people, how he's been treated unfairly, threatened, insulted, attacked, and more, just for being a black man. Then says You know my daughter can be crazy. I say I know. We talk about women, and even laugh some. When the second bottle is done, he calls for the others and tells them he thinks I'm nuts for wanting to marry Bambi and get into her mess, but if that's what we want, he won't stop us. We go to meet with her pastor the next day but are told he's been transferred, by an embarrassed young priest just arrived from Ireland, who says he can't marry us.

54

Bambi wants to convert to Judaism and get a rabbi to marry us. We argue about it til my leave is up. Back in South Carolina I find the locker in my cubicle ransacked. One of the good old boys says Buncha colored boys carried yall's stuff out, figgered they's yall's friends. Smirk smirk. My record player and Paul Sargent suit are gone. But they left the broken guitar back I retrieved from the garbage and made a collage on of *DOWNBEAT* photos of jazz icons. When Bambi gives up her idea of converting to Judaism, we return to our previous plan. She goes to an unwed mothers home in Newark for the last several weeks before the baby is due.

55

I come out of a blackout in a car with two black dudes who say I offered to buy them an after hours drink. We go to an old shack, where an ancient black lady in her nightie pours us each a glass of what looks like water with dark specks in it. One cat calls it DOGBITE. It burns my mouth and tongue and throat. I always marvel at how soft a fall feels when I get knocked out, a slow motion release onto a pile of pillows while sparkly little colored lights pop in my head. With DOGBITE, I just feel on fire before I collapse and wake up lying by the side of the road a sheriff's deputy nudging me with the tip of his boot. There are more and more nights like that.

56

Some young black men overturn a bus in the Nickeltown night, after one of them refuses to sit in the rear. It doesn't make the national or even local news. Another night, a confrontation between me with some black friends and a gang of rednecks outside THE GHANA gets broken up by deputies. My commander tells me the sheriff wants me out of South Carolina. Asked where I'd like to be assigned, I tell him New York, not believing he cares. But the next day I get orders to report on June first to Fort Monmouth, an Army base with a small airfield on the Jersey shore, less than an hour from New York. It's April but they tell me to Leave now.

THE JERSEY SHORE SONNETS

"Are you right there, Michael, are you right? Do you think you can hang on by sitting tight?"

—James Joyce (riffing on the lyrics to Irish composer Percy French's song)

1

I visit Bambi at the home for unwed mothers
in Newark, and my sister Joan in South Orange
pregnant too, praying this one won't end like
the others, in miscarriage or stillbirth from
the diabetes she's had since childhood. I stay
at Cliff's until I have to report to the fort and
buy my first car to visit Bambi in, an old
Morris Minor with a radio bolted upside down
to the bottom of the dashboard, tubes exposed.
After the tubes fall out, to compensate I glue
poems by Diane di Prima, Ray Bremser, and
Philip Lamantia from *THE BEATS*, along with
photos from *DOWNBEAT*, all over the inside
of the car, so it's like riding inside a collage.

2

When I turn twenty-one, Jersey friends throw
me a party in East Orange where Little Robert,
eyes filled with tears after too many beers, says
This crazy motherfucker ain't never gonna see
twenty-two. Bambi gives birth at Saint Michael's
down the street from my old all-boys school in
Newark. In a ward with mostly white women,
their husbands are nice to us, everyone in that
first flush of new baby pride and taking me for
the dad. That doesn't last. My sister loses her baby
there weeks later. Bambi gives hers up and catches
a bus to Asbury Park, from where I drive us to
Belmar and its ethnic beaches where 18th Ave, the
Irish one, experiences its first interracial couple.

3

People stare as I lead Bambi to the water's edge
to spread a G.I. blanket on the sand. Later rolling
ourselves up in it, we defiantly make love. She
expects a fight or the cops to be called. But no
one does anything more than glare at us when we
get up to leave. While I'm at work Bambi hangs
with a black brother and his sister she met on
the bus. I want her to stay away from him. She
says she just wants to be free, near me, and not
be told who she can or can't see. Stopped at
a red light, we get into a fight. She struggles to
pull the engagement ring off her finger, while
I accuse her of faking, to keep it. The car door
slams behind her, breaking my life in half.

4

I get so drunk, I total my car in a blackout, come
to in my bunk covered with cuts. The mechanic
calls my Morris Minor a little tank as he puts it
back together. But no one can do that for my life.
After one night shift, my replacement finds me
passed out drunk, head smashed into the teletype
machine that sends weather reports. There'd been
no flights, so no accidents. My pay's docked for
the broken glass, and I lose my pass for a while.
Coming out of another night's blackout, I'm out-
side our barracks staring at a brother threatening me
with a piece of pipe, both in our G.I. boxers. I say
What the fuck man? He points to the broken bottle
in my hand. I drop it. He tosses the piece of pipe.

5

My friend says I passed out drunk, late for my
night shift, and when our brand new lieutenant
came to fetch me, unable to rouse me he picked
up the end of my cot and dropped it. I jumped up
fists flying and knocked him down. To keep me
from making things worse, my friend pushed
me out the door, where I picked up the broken
bottle, so he grabbed the piece of pipe. The new
lieutenant, embarrassed, split. My man urges me
to get to my job before the new lewie calls the APs.
Next day when the new lieutenant tries to bring
me up on charges, our captain says he better not,
cause the lewie didn't stop me from going to work
the night before still loaded and a danger to the job.

6

Years later I'll tell the story of me and the new
lieutenant, at the 20th-Century Fox Commissary
in L.A. to David Milch and Bill Clark. Clark,
who'd been an officer in Nam, will claim I'd
never get away with punching an officer under
any circumstances, though this happened before
his time. I won't argue, admitting I was drunk
and high a lot so maybe I had it wrong. But I
knew it's all true. Like the dawn I awake to a
farmer rapping on my window, more surprised
than angry to find me asleep in my Morris Minor
in the middle of his cornfield. He helps me push
it out of the corn and back to the highway, just
feet away from that big bridge in the Amboys.

7

At my Grandma Dempsey's Belmar bungalow, in the summers of my boyhood, there was a family, almost as big as ours, who lived in a small house behind us and were what city folks called clam diggers, year-round locals. I fell in love with Charlotte, the little girl in the family, despite her curly, bright orangey red hair. I was fascinated by her brothers and her, all tougher than me and much wilder. They'd squat and shit when they felt the urge in what we called woods, but was just a vacant lot full of scrub pine. When I was seven, they all moved to the actual woods and I didn't see her again, until a decade later much to my surprise.

8

One hot summer day, when I was still in high school, Charlie drove his crew to Asbury Park in his new used Buick convertible. Stuck in traffic, as the only white guy I volunteered to get us sodas at a counter we could see just inside a nearby pavilion. The girl behind it had bright, orangey, curly hair, and a voluptuous body her white uniform couldn't hide. I asked when she got off work and showed up to ride the carousel with her, where she revealed she was Charlotte. That summer in the back of Spanish Harry's car we made love in ways I never had before, kissing her soft white skin everywhere, including under the bright, curly, orangey red hair down there.

9

After the breakup with Bambi, I look Charlotte up one drunken night. Still living with her family and dating some guy from the backwoods, when she sees me at her door she steps out into the dark. We drive to Belmar, find a spot by the water where we can't be seen from the boardwalk, lay down in the sand, and make love, her gazing up at the sky over my shoulder as she whispers My God the stars. Sitting in her pickup truck one night weeks later, Charlotte tells me she's going to marry her back-woods boyfriend. She says she knows she'll always come second to my writing, or music, or memories of Bambi. She wants someone she'll always be number one to. I'll never see her again.

10

When Martin Luther King gives his I HAVE A DREAM speech, I remind my friends and family that I predicted a wave of racial equality would be coming, that I'd ride triumphantly to history's shore. Not long after that, while working in the tower on The Fort Monmouth airfield, I watch as army buses, and troops with rifles at the ready, surround the runway. As a copter lands in the middle of the circle they make, the phone rings. It's a *DAILY NEWS* reporter who offers me fifty bucks to tell him what I see, as Joe Vilachi, the Mafia informer, is taken off the helicopter. I get the reporter to up the ante to a hundred before I hang up.

11

On a perfectly clear Fall day, heading back to Fort Monmouth, I watch as other cars on The Garden State Parkway veer onto the shoulder and stop, the drivers not getting out, just sitting there. At the toll booth, the man says The president's been shot. As I drive on, more cars pull off the road. I can see their drivers weeping. Back in the barracks we stay in the rec room watching the black-and-white TV, tension in the room like static. When they name Lee Harvey Oswald, I watch the black guys hold their breath, hoping that means redneck not spade, and every muscle in their faces relax, when he turns out to be white.

12

From the institution she's in for a suicide attempt, Lee writes she'll come visit when she gets out. Before she can, I'm reassigned to a base in Washington state. The night before I split, I visit Dolores tending bar where TONY PASTOR'S used to be on West Third, now a jazz joint with Cecil Taylor soloing on piano. She doesn't dig his radically dissonant improvising. Later she pays for a hotel room off Washington Square where, looking up at me after making love, her eyes bright in the dark of the room and her face, she says Oh why don't you marry her. After I'm gone, she and Bambi become friends, then roommates.

THE SPOKANE SONNETS

"What doesn't come to me from me has come to the wrong address."

—Samuel Beckett

1

My first night in what the locals pronounce
Spo-can, I look for a woman to help me
forget Bambi. A banner over the main drag
announces: *WELCOME TO JOHN BIRCH
COUNTRY.* The bars are all white, but I'm
not particular this night. Entering one, I
catch the feeling of The Old West. The long
hardwood bar, a dark presence down the left
side of the room, is from the 1800s the bar-
tender says. At one table are four young
white chicks, one lovely. When a slow tune
comes on the box, I ask her to dance. She
looks to her friends who seem to approve.
Holding her in my arms, I think of Bambi.

2

Where you from? The Apple. She gives me a
quizzical look. New York. She says she guessed
Out East from my odd outfit: new tight collar-
less jacket, new pointy-toed boots of many
buckles. The song ends, I say I'll be right back.
Two wiry white guys follow me into the john.
One says the girl I danced with is his ex-wife. I
say Ex means she's free to dance with whoever
she wants. He hits me. I can't take them both
so drop to the floor, as if his punch knocked me
down, though it glanced off the side of my head.
The other gives me a few quick kicks. After they
leave, I get up, dust myself off, comb my hair,
and walk right out of the men's room and the bar.

3

In a big old roadhouse built out of huge stones,
with an elevated stage on which a local band
wails *Maggie used to carry my books to school
Maggie was a good old girl* to a roaring crowd,
a dark haired country girl, looking like Patsy
Kline to me, says Let's go back to my place.
A guy following us out says She's with me.
She says No I'm with him. He hits me over the
head with his beer bottle, but when I don't go
down he goes back inside. To get friends, she
says as she pulls me into her car. At her tiny
pad, just as I'm about to enter her she warns
me that she has the clap. I assure her that I
have The Luck of the Irish. And this time I do.

4

The USO advertises *TONIGHT THE BEATLES
ON THE ED SULLIVAN SHOW*. Up a flight of
stairs is a large TV in a big open room full of
white teenage girls vibrating with anticipation.
Waiting for the show, I slow dance with one
to a 45. An old lady rushes over with a ruler to
ensure the space between our bodies is at least
six inches. About to split, a young cat with a
hound dog face walks up to me and asks You
a musician? I nod. Jazz, he guesses. I nod again.
He's Jimmy Dunaway, nineteen, a drummer air-
man from the base. With his tightly curled hair,
skin darker than my Irish parchment, and thick-
er lips, I assume he has some African ancestry.

5

If Jimmy has Negro blood he doesn't know it. He talks like a typical Southern good ol' boy sentimental about the Civil War and the Old South his daddy told him all about. After Ed Sullivan, a triumph for The Beatles but to us just pop adolescent girl stuff, though secretly impressed, we bar hop til I can find a black joint, by then so skunky drunk when we get angry looks I climb up on the bar and do some rhymes, what older black folks call toasting: I might be too thin to win but ain't too light to fight or too lean to be mean. An old ploy to distract people til it's too late to battle and I'm accepted as a crazy Paddy.

6

I form a jazz trio with Jimmy and another cat from the base, a short black dude people call Rabbi cause he always wears a long dark rain-coat when not in uniform, even on the band-stand. Sometimes Rabbi doesn't show so Jimmy and me play as a duo. One early AM after a gig while eating breakfast at DENNY'S we're ambushed by a voluptuous blonde with sparkling blue eyes. I flirt til she invites me back to her place. As we undress in the dark I realize there's someone else in her bed. When I hesitate she says Haven't you ever made love to a woman in front of her husband before? I lie and say Sure all the time. Her name is Sandy, and his is Billy.

7

While we make love his eyes watch us in the dark. I don't think Dirty Old Man, cause he's only a little older than me. In the morning over pancakes they explain what an open marriage is. They believe in free love. Their pad is a hang-out for other free souls, like Jewel, a sixteen-year-old runaway blond, with an infant who sleeps in an empty drawer on the living room floor next to the couch Jewel sleeps on. Her family threw her out when she got pregnant. Sandy's sister Roxie stops by after high school, the first teenager I ever saw with died tar black hair dressed like she's on her way to a funeral. She's also very bright and precociously cynical.

8

Billy works for Duncan yo-yos traveling the country showcasing his yo-yo skills with the usual tricks and a few spectacular ones of his own. At parties he uses two yo-yos and their strings to illustrate unique sexual scenarios or he leans a quarter from the top of my ear to the side of my head, then flicks the quarter off with his yo-yo, not touching my ear or my hair. He hires me as part of his stage act, playing piano behind his tricks, ending with the coin on my ear bit. He's handsome in the manner of old movie stars, with slicked-back dark hair, smoky eyes, and the wisp of a smile exuding confidence and some secret deviltry going on.

9

A white guy in my outfit, Rick, first Southern Californian I've known, invites me to join him in a pad in town, against regulations. We keep beds in the barracks and show up for inspections. I'm assigned to the Spokane airport to assist the civilians, so living in an apartment seems right. Rick is thin, with short, dark, PETER GUNN hair, a smile more like a smirk, and different taste. But he has a car and a reel-to-reel tape recorder he tapes music off the radio on, like The Beach Boys, whose songs I dismiss as trite teenage jive, but later get as Bach chorale WASP soul harmonies. Rick pays for food and keeps the refrigerator full of beer, and I pay half the rent.

10

I never learn why the Air Force pays me to work at the civilian airport, but it makes my life easier. I rarely have to deal with the usual petty military restrictions, instead I work with the airport weatherman, or alone in the runway tower recording the weather, or on days when there isn't much, watching a coyote family grow among the tumbleweeds at the edge of the runway, til the day I'm enjoying the new litter of coyote pups rough-housing, through my binoculars, and spy a sheriff's deputy walking toward them pull out his gun suddenly and start shooting. The mom gets away but he massacres all the pups.

11

One morning around dawn, working in the office with the tall, bald, bespectacled, jokey, civilian weatherman, I watch a new kind of plane, a Lear jet, land and in a few minutes a guy who looks a lot like Danny Kaye comes in. The weatherman grabs him around the neck and makes jokes at his expense, so I figure it's just a lookalike. As I watch the man leave, and still have my eye on the empty doorway, he sticks his head back in, makes a funny Danny Kaye face at me, and disappears. I say That's Danny Kaye! The weatherman replies Who'd ya think it was? I say The way you were acting I thought you knew him. He says I do know him, from TV. I only know him from his movies.

12

Linda is a country girl from what she says is THE VALLEY OF THE GREEN GIANT where they grow the peas and other stuff the Giant is the symbol of. She worked the fields with migrant farmhands before moving to Spokane and a job as a motel maid. She's as tall as me and probably stronger from all her hard labor. She shares a crib in a house on the other side of our block with a more sophisticated girl, the original target of my interest who chose a handsome white vibe player over me. His trio won the base talent contest over mine in the jazz category. But I won the comedy trophy playing and singing, solo and drunkenly, Jon Hendricks's hip paean *GIMME THAT WINE.*

13

Linda stops by one hot summer day in a
bathing suit, slowly removing it after we
end up in my bedroom where she slides
her legs over the edge of the bed and
I take it into my mouth. So small. Like
the tip of a baby's finger. I've been here
before with Charlotte and Bambi, but
this is different. I don't get off, just watch
as she moves like surfing in slow motion,
and begins to breathe for both of us. That
night she returns claiming her roommate
and the vibe player are keeping her awake.
In my room she changes into a flimsy filmy
nightie thing and slides between my sheets.

14

I wake to find Linda sitting silently at the window looking out at the trees as dawn breaks. We find some canned food for breakfast. She tells me back home her friends call her Snaggletooth, for the broken incisor and the ways other teeth compete for space and angles in her mouth. We're still eating, her in her negligee, me in my GI boxers, when Sandy unexpectedly drops by. After Linda goes to dress, Sandy says she understands why I'm attracted to Linda's body. But that's not it. After Linda splits Sandy confesses that she's in love with Jewel, the teen with a baby who lives with her and Billy. This isn't the first time someone confesses their secrets to me.

15

I spy a black-haired beauty in the backyard of the house next door. With two long braids hanging over her shoulders, she nurses a baby while looking up at me in the window. We stare at each other often after that. One day a knock on my door is her, inviting me to a small party. Her name is Kateerie. Everyone calls her Kat, a native American from a Mid-west reservation. But I see Irish in the impish sparkle of her dark eyes. Her white artist hus-band's name is Valiant. His mother added Von as his middle name so it sounds like he's European royalty. He looks the part with his pale skin, ink black hair, and Van Dyke chin.

16

Val's friend Hugh painted a portrait of Val's mom naked from the waist up, displaying the results of a mastectomy in lurid detail. She writes short stories under male pen names. I realize I've read a cowboy story of hers in a Western mag I found in the weather tower. She shows me her system for keeping track of where her stories are sent and rejected or accepted, all dated on index cards. I adopt it for the writing I constantly send out but keep getting back. Val's friend Don, a quiet, balding post office clerk nicknamed, ironically, Mad Dog, only owns records of Beethoven's music, turning me on to him with an album of his piano pieces for my twenty-second birthday.

17

Roy and Karen are married college students. A big bright guy, he writes Beckett inspired plays. The son of a sergeant, he's lived all over. Karen, pretty and smart, makes pottery and art. They say what sounds to me like Chow whenever they leave anywhere. Roy is my first close college-educated writer friend. I argue with him about books I haven't read, then go to the base library or used book store to see if I'm right. He and Karen live in a rented cabin on Fish Lake with water you have to pump, their only neighbors Hugh and his lady, til Val and Kat rent the farmhouse across the road to raise chickens.

18

Tom Wilson, another white college kid, sings and plays guitar and harmonica, a la Woody Guthrie, at PRIDE'S CASTLE, the coffee house Sandy runs as a refuge for Spokane's misfits. Tom invites me to a party where I name who's playing what on his jazz albums, our friendship cemented when we both laugh with delight at the same riff in a sax solo and slap hands. I learn he's the president of his class and The Young Democrats, also captain of The ROTC and the track team. His beautiful fiancé, Ramona, is the granddaughter of the last chief of the Colville tribe on a nearby reservation.

19

I sold my Morris Minor to my ex-nun sister Irene
when I went West, but after relying on others for
rides I buy an early '50s Willys with those little
attempts at some kind of fins and a paint job that
looks like an oil slick. It gets me where I want
to go, and sometimes when drunk where I don't.
Like at 3AM after heavy boozing going to see a
white nurse I dated before Linda. I ring the bell,
bang on the door, yell threats against the hospital,
her boss, anyone, then run back to the Willys
and honk the horn. Windows open. Someone
yells Go home and sober up. Windows close.
I quiet down, get back in the car and drive
home, *confused*, as I'll write in a journal later.

20

Bill Tandy, an older black cat, maybe thirty,
reminds me of Destiny, same sweet smile
and gentle soul. One night after Sandy closes
PRIDE'S CASTLE she lets the regulars stay.
Tandy's date is a white stripper, so me and
Jimmy play *HARLEM NOCTURNE* and
she does her routine. When it ends we keep
playing til dawn. Rick makes a quick run to
get his reel-to-reel to capture two hours of
our best improvising, including Jimmy with
one stick not missing a beat as he swigs a
beer, puts the can down on his snare, picks
up the other stick and keeps playing around
and on the can, without ever spilling a drop.

21

Roland Chase is very dark and very big and married to a short white woman. When they have a baby it fits into one of his enormous hands. We meet one night at THE RED LION, the only bar in Spokane truly integrated. But no black single women my age. It specializes in honey-dipped fried chicken I could eat every night for the rest of my life. One night, drunk and looking for a fight, when a white couple sits down at a table I grab some peanuts from the bowl on the bar and begin throwing one at a time at the man. He glares at me. I growl Got a problem motherfucker? And throw another but miss and hit Roland.

22

When Roland stands up, it's like he might block out all the light in the room. I get up too and go to him before he comes to me. As he says Let's step outside, I step right up into his chest, bend my head back and staring up at his face say Okay man but dig, if you kick my ass ain't nobody gonna be surprised, but if I kick yours you ain't never gonna be able to show your face around here no more. As I step back, he bursts out laughing at my cocky attitude, slaps me on the back almost knocking me on my ass, and offers to buy me a drink. I sit down with him and his friends and we're tight from then on.

23

In the Willys with Jimmy one night, I go through a red light into a one way street going the wrong way head-on into a taxi. When the cops arrive I have the cabbie over the hood of his cab, blaming him, Jimmy later tells me. I'm in a blackout so don't remember that, or the cops dragging me to jail. In court the judge holds up a card I wrote my information on for the cabbie, and asks me to read out loud what I wrote. Unable to decipher what looks like chicken scratchings, I shake my head, chuckle, and say That sure looks like my handwriting alright. The judge laughs and passes it to the cop and prosecutor. They laugh too. Then the judge suspends my license for a few months.

24

Despite my drinking getting worse, I keep writing stories and poems daily and sending them to magazines and agents. Novels too. Thirteen since my first. After my twenty-second birthday, in a drunken rage at the rejections piling up, I burn the novels in a barrel in the backyard. With no idea how to interpret rejection letters, I react to them all with equal disappointment. Some suggest changes and trying again, like Sterling Lord who I later find out is Kerouac's agent. He asks me to rewrite and resend one of my novels. But I still believe that re-writing is selling out, so I burn that manuscript too.

25

It's three AM when I drunkenly wake Linda and her pretty roommate. They have to get up early for work. Trying to get me to leave, Linda points to her clock radio saying Look what time it is Michael. I throw it to the floor and stomp on it, til it's a broken mess, then point at it yelling That's what fucking time it is! When a friend of hers from THE VALLEY OF THE GREEN GIANT comes to visit, the tough little country boy lets me know he don't like me and challenges me to a fight. He seems ready and willing to kill me if he has to, so I back down. After he leaves town I get drunk and start a fight with a stranger not so scary.

26

Jimmy tells me Linda's too country for a city boy like me, I'm too smart and she's too uneducated, I'm too cool for her, she's more his type than mine. I ask him if he's fallen for her. He says he feels she'll be happier with him than with me. We talk to her about it. She agrees Jimmy's a better choice for her, though still looks longingly at me. Too drunk to figure it out, I let them. They decide to marry. Tom Wilson and his native American princess, Ramona, set the date for their wedding too. Della writes me she's moved to Harlem, has a pad of her own and wants me to come live with her.

27

I'm working the graveyard shift at the airport the night PRIDE'S CASTLE is raided. The cops, interrogating everyone, tell Jimmy to let me know they're watching me. The next day's paper and TV news makes it look like a big dope bust, with FBI informants. To beef up the numbers they include all the arrests made that night. They book Tandy for an open pint bottle of bourbon, and grill Sandy and Billy separately to get them to implicate others in something more than after-hours boozing in a coffee house. They want the place shut down for being what the newspaper calls: *a beatnik nuisance.*

28

The cops tell Sandy they know what she's been up to. She thinks they mean her and Jewel, so admits to what she thinks is a sympathetic jail matron that she's in love with Jewel, revealing all about her and Billy's free love scene. Jewel's still underage, mother or not, unwanted by anyone else in her family, or society, or not. Sandy and Billy go to jail, Billy to be kept in solitary for over a year. Rick splits to visit his folks in California. I stock up on booze and beer and do my drinking in the apartment, afraid to venture out to a bar and have the cops grab me. All that's left from PRIDE'S CASTLE is Rick's tape.

29

I call Della to come to me. She asks where
Spokane is, laughs when I tell her, saying
You crazy, fool. I call other black women in
my little black book. Moving to Spokane
doesn't appeal to them either. I call not-black
Lee and ask her to join me. She says she helps
run a puppet show on Fantasy Island in Lake
Erie and it will take a week to get out of that.
A friend is driving to California soon after,
she'll come then. Before I can respond, she
says she'll skip the ride, use her savings to
fly out and be with me by the end of the week.
We talk for hours til I'm too drunk to hold
the phone or make sense of the conversation.

30

I wake up hung over with a vague memory of
phone calls, throw down my morning shot to
calm my nerves and decide to call Lee back
to try and get out of whatever commitments
I made the night before. Then I realize I can
go see what she's really like and at the same
time escape the heat from the Spokane police.
So when she tells me she already checked on
a flight, I say No baby stay there, I'll come to
you and we'll dig what happens. I put in for a
week's leave, get two hundred from the credit
union and a round trip ticket to Buffalo. The
night before I leave, one of our Navy boats is
shot at by the North Vietnamese in Tonkin Bay.

31

I don't remember what Lee looks like but have an idea of her life from her letters. Like riding horses bareback by a lake, to me a rich kid luxury. I picture the lake on her family's estate. I know she works, but as a puppeteer and as a volunteer in a hospital. Sounds like rich girl pastimes. And she's a student at The University of Buffalo, a high class education to me. When I got kicked out of Saint Bonaventure's, she wrote that her father could get me a job in Buffalo. I'm assuming he has a position of power there. So when the airport taxi pulls up in front of a little tract house in Tonawanda I say You got the wrong address.

32

When I ring the doorbell, a small dark-haired woman I can't get a good look at wraps her arms around me as if afraid I might run away. A foot shorter than me, her face buried in the front of my uniform coat, I hug her back, wondering what's happening. Before I can ask, she grabs my hand pulling me behind her to the basement of the tiny house and her father's workshop where, I learn, he makes devices for dentists, and jewelry for his wife and two daughters out of leftover dental hardware. He too is short with black hair but has a pronounced limp as he paces his lab, arguing with his oldest daughter.

33

Lee's dad, Elmer, talking out of one side of his mouth in a Ralph Kramden working-class lug style, finally says Well if you bananas wanna get married I can't stop you. I'm thinking What bananas? He asks Lee about some guy she's engaged to, me thinking She's engaged? It goes on like that for a while, me bewildered while trying to get a good look at her but not wanting to stare, having trouble focusing after all the plane-ride booze. After a while she leads me out of there to a nearby playground where we sit side by side on swings and talk about who we are, including our lover experiences. But I still can't get a good solid look at her.

34

Lee tells me about an older guy, a ski bum she calls him, who taught her more about sex than anyone else, an old man in his thirties, maybe even forty. And of another Michael, who published a poem of hers under his own name in the University of Buffalo literary magazine and was exposed. He later apologized and they've become friends again. And the guy she's engaged to, who's a pre-med student she said yes to cause her folks liked him, but she's already told him it's over. I tell her of my lovers, and how I still love Bambi, which she already knows from my letters.

35

Lee is the most understanding woman I know, in her letters. Smart, creative, and hip, her foxy little figure recalls Della's, the most physically satisfying sexual partner I've ever had. So when a friend of Lee's drives us to get blood tests and a marriage license, seeing it as a new adventure I go. That night we hit a bar with, like OBIES, queers, poets, artists, bikers, junkies, boozers, and potheads. When her Michael, a big bearded Jewish guy palms fifty into my hand as a wedding gift as he shakes it, it pisses me off, hurting my drunken pride, and for stealing Lee's poem whether she's forgiven him or not. I storm out to wander Buffalo's dark streets in a blackout.

36

After searching with friends Lee finds me, gets me back to her house and into her little sister's bed while they sleep in hers. Only ten, her sister tells me next day that the neighborhood kids are teasing her about Lee marrying a hood. Lee's sister is fair like their mother, Emily Jane, a country girl with city ambitions who I am certain feels trapped in her role as suburban housewife the second I look into her eyes and recognize my own kind of ambitious self-conscious appetite for more. A small, birdlike woman, attractive in a country kind of way with a protruding upper lip, a la Gloria Grahame, she plays guitar, and taught Lee to too.

37

We spend an afternoon making out for the first time, among the sand dunes on Lake Erie where Lee rides the rented horses I had thought she owned. She tells me how as a girl she'd sometimes come home from school to find her mother passed out on the kitchen floor, drunk. That stopped after her mom got a part time job. And how her dad's shorter leg got that way as a boy, from sliding into a gutter third base in a game of stick ball on a Buffalo street. In WWII the military accepted him as a noncombatant and taught him to make dental devices. Lee was born on a Naval base in 1943. She and Elmer are less fair skinned than her sister and mother, but his eyes are light blue like theirs, Lee's a penetrating green.

38

The ROAD VULTURES, Buffalo's HELL'S ANGELS, throw Lee a party to celebrate her about-to-be marriage. While Lee dances with her pretty blonde Maid of Honor, I dig Lee's shapely body and sensuous moves, surprised the bikers' 45s are mostly R&B. One little cat doesn't dig my spade slang or jazzman style so gets in my face. I figure I have to take him on, but Tommy Bell, their leader, steps in, apologizing for him, saying the cat's all fucked up on speed. The artist of the gang, Spain Rodriquez, gives us a cartoon drawing of himself on his hog, and a Zippo he engraved our initials entwined on with the point of his knife.

39

When I call my mother to invite her and my family to the wedding, she asks Is she…? Before she finishes I say She's white. She says That's not what I was going to ask, is she…? I interrupt again She's Catholic. That's NOT what I was going to ask Is she…? No, she's not pregnant. THAT'S NOT WHAT I WAS GOING TO ASK! But no more questions. At the motel she, my dad, sisters, and Joe stay at, they all want to know if Lee knows about Bambi. They're sure Lee's pregnant and that's why the wedding is rushed and unexpected. I can't explain that I think it's a daring act, like a work of art, another sign of my creative genius.

40

At the wedding in the grammar school gym, the church still being built, Spanish Harry, my best man cause he could make the gig, who had taken Elmer on the night before in a shot contest and lost, rises from the kneeler beside me to mumble as he heads to the men's room Sorry Lal. Still under construction it's more like a cubicle, so everyone can hear him barf while the priest finishes the ceremony. When we leave the party after the wedding, Lee's maternal grandpa, a short but wide old farmer, pulls me aside, I think to warn me to take care of Lee, but instead he growls If she gives you any trouble just give her a good whack.

41

My old man and brother-in-law came in separate cars so I could use one to drive to a honeymoon motel after we visit Lee's farm cousins out in the countryside. They treat me with mild disdain in my too tight pants and pointy-toed city slicker boots and shades. Her uncle takes us to his cow barn to show Lee new milking machines, leading me behind the cows as he explains it all. When a cow takes a big dump as we pass and it splashes onto my cool cat boots and pants, he can't stop laughing. At the motel I drink my way through dinner and the show, two talented Korean sisters singing, dancing, and doing contortionist gymnastics.

42

After we make love, Lee takes me in her arms as if I were a child. That has never happened to me before. She's the tiny one. I push her away. Next morning, the drive to the city is quiet. In upper Manhattan we get stuck in a traffic jam, the sidewalks overflowing with people. I roll down the window to ask What's goin' on? It's the funeral for Goodman and Schwerner, young New York white men killed in Mississippi with Chaney, a young Southern black man, for attempting to register black voters. At a record shop on St. Mark's I scat, note for note, Nat Adderly's solo on *THE NEARNESS OF YOU*, for Lee.

43

At OBIES, Sblibby gets salty with me when he meets Lee. He's friends with Delores now and thinks I should have married her if not Bambi even though she and Bambi aren't friends anymore. When Dolores shows up, she breaks a bottle, threatening to cut me, but I manage to calm her down. Cal says Bambi's living with another white guy. He, Mel, DeWitt, and Cliff throw Lee and me a party. Later in bed at Cliff's Lee says I turn into someone else around my friends, especially my speech. Around her family I controlled my street black hip slang that even Bambi had trouble understanding. Lee worries she doesn't know who I really am.

44

Cliff takes us to a party at a friend's from the U.N. who asked him to bring some Village types. I argue with African princes and European dudes about the USA, defending it despite all I dislike, while Lee is passed out in a bedroom. Next day we go to a party my family throws us in our little house in Jersey and visit Maureen at her crib in Orange. We get into such an intense discussion that when Mo goes to pee she leaves her bathroom door open so we can keep talking. It impresses me as amazingly brave and hip to be so unselfconscious and natural with friends. But Lee later makes clear she saw it as sexual provocation aimed at me and is angrily jealous in a way I've never experienced.

45

On the plane ride to Spokane, we get better
acquainted. Lee, a twenty-one-year-old
Merit Scholar, fencing and skiing champ, and
published poet who plays guitar and sings.
And me, her twenty-two-year-old husband she
hardly knows outside of letters. I'll soon learn
she's also an accomplished artist who can
paint miniature scenes on blown-out eggs to
make personal Christmas ornaments, and an
amazing calligrapher, cook, and seamstress.
I only know her from her letters too, which
her behavior has already begun to contradict.
But it feels cooly adult to greet friends waiting
at Rick's and my place, as a married couple.

46

Rick isn't happy I've come back with a wife.
When asked to play the tape of the after hours
jam session at PRIDE'S CASTLE I told Lee
about, he says he taped over it. The smart
dark-haired girl I turned on to him breaks up
with him over it. Other friends never include
him in again. My first night back, in response
to Tonkin Bay I'm ordered to the base to make
Top Secret weather maps of Russia and China.
Like the SAC base in *DR. STRANGELOVE* we
always have bombers in the air heading there
so if we're attacked by their nuclear weapons,
even if the USA is destroyed, we'll still have
planes on their way to drop our nukes on them.

47

Hunting for a new pad in an old building that reminds me of a New York tenement with its dark dingy hallway, when the old man who answers the manager's door goes for his wife we hear him say The wife's colored. It's Lee's olive skin. She's angry that I get a kick out of this. We find a place in the basement of a big old house on Chestnut Street owned by an old farm couple who've turned each floor into an apartment. Ours is half the basement, the other half has the furnace and hot water heater. The first floor has another military couple. A handsome Air Policeman, his blonde wife, and infant Lee begins babysitting after we move in.

48

When I finally get a sober look at Lee in daylight I can see part of her lip is collapsed and there's a scar from around her ear to under her chin, where a knot of veins create an almost blue hue. I make a lame joke about the comic book hero *IRON JAW* she does not find funny. After being in two car crashes, she quit driving and had a series of operations to fix her face, but ended them when the doc died halfway through, she says. After that she let friends and family know they and everyone else will just have to live with the way she looks. I'm proud of her stand, always leaning toward the natural in any conception of how things should be. If that's what she wants, it's cool with me.

49

The first night I take Lee to THE RED LION
a drunk old lady leans across the table we're
sharing to say Oh you poor dearie, did you just
come from the dentist? Lee just stares her into
submissive silence. I watch her do that often.
People turn red and walk away after inquiring
about her well being, based on their perception
of the slight deformity in her face. Others
find her beautiful including, often, me. Her
intensely green eyes seem to challenge you
to dig them. Most people can later recall
the moment they first saw Lee, they were so
struck by her physical presence and style, a
little bit sexy Beat, a little in your face unique.

50

Lee plays me songs she knows on guitar, and
I play her songs I know on the piano we rent.
When Jimmy and Rabbi come for rehearsals
or other musicians stop by to jam, I encourage
her to join in, which she sometimes does on a
tambourine or bongos but never her guitar. For
some people I can get her to play on her own,
even sing along to her strumming, but always a
country or folk song. She has records by music
makers I know, like Monk and Miles, but more
I don't, like the Carter family, Ian and Sylvia,
Buffy Saint Marie, and Dylan, whose new *THE
TIMES THEY ARE A-CHANGIN'* awes me with
its unique genius, though I still doubt his story.

51

I suggest Lee sign up for college classes but she chooses to stay home, throwing herself into housework. Full of animosity toward the world at large, she wants to create a cocoon for us to hide from it in. She blames this attitude on men like the one who exposed himself to her on her way home from elementary school, or the ones who later made unwanted attempts to have sex with her, or commented on her style or figure as provocative. Elmer had wanted a son, so he treated Lee like one, teaching her to hunt deer with a gun and skin and butcher them, calling her by her androgynous middle name. But he also makes jokes about how large her bra is.

52

Some mornings, after a night of hard drinking, I awake to find Lee scrubbing the floor on her knees or baking bread, or cleaning or sewing. We go out most nights to clubs and bars where I'm playing or friends are. At THE RED LION one night, two older black men get into a razor fight. When one slashes the other's cheek, the red glowing like neon on his dark skin, the man who's cut falls across our table. I shove him off and go on with my drinking. Another night at an outdoor party a pale unpublished novelist who considers himself a rugged Westerner, to prove a point in an argument, shoots a beer bottle out of my hand, frightening Lee. But I'm so drunk it doesn't even faze me.

53

Lee leans over to kiss me while I'm writing a story, and the words fly out of my head. I stand up and walk out, spending the next several hours wandering around Spokane thinking about the dilemma of having someone around when you're writing. When I get back, she has been crying for a while. She says she wasn't sure where I went, or even if I would ever come back. I tell her I can take my little portable typewriter and throw it in the garbage and never write again, or she can never bother me again when I'm writing. She chooses the latter, but soon starts complaining about the girly magazines I send my stories to.

54

I come home from work to find Lee sobbing. When I ask why, she hands me a photo album she found in the closet. I wasn't hiding it. It's one of my most prized possessions, with Bambi's high school photo and pics of other old friends, mostly female, most of them black. I point out they represent sweet memories to me, but Lee expresses her fear and jealousy so fiercely, I carry the album out to where the furnace is and open the little door in it and throw the photo album in. As soon as it leaves my fingers I'm profoundly sorry. I know I'll always regret it, but I pretend it's no big deal, as Lee pretends it isn't what she really wanted.

55

Tom and Ramona have a big wedding I'm so bombed at I won't remember it. They leave for their honeymoon in the old Willys I sell them after I buy a two-toned '55 Pontiac automatic from a sergeant who convinces me it's more appropriate for a married man. Jimmy and Linda marry too, with me as best man, in a Coeur d'Alene, Idaho, dusty little secular chapel presided over by a woman in a graduation gown playing the wedding march on a record player, scratching the disc when she lifts the needle off as we reach the mock altar where she tells Linda to remove her chewing gum.

56

We see The Kingston Trio and Miriam Makeba in a new arena. Lee knows the guy who replaced one of the originals, so after the show introduces me to him backstage. He, in turn, introduces us to Miriam Makeba, tiny like Lee but black and beautiful in a uniquely African way that overwhelms me. Lee gets angrily jealous. When I read her a new rejection letter for an old story I wrote about a paddy cat and spade chick waking in a dry fountain in Washington Square, in which the editor accuses me of imitating Kerouac, all Lee focuses on is that the story is about me and Bambi, getting so angry she swears: If I ever see her on the street in New York I'll cut her heart out!

57

Despite our troubles, we make love every night. If not, Lee makes me feel her disappointment. As time passes our lovemaking becomes ever more satisfying, creating a closeness that begins to translate into the rest of our relationship. She writes love notes for my lunch bag or leaves them hidden around our pad for me to find. I begin doing the same. We write poems together too. I write a song called *NIGHTLEE*. Alone at home we become tight and right. But Lee does not like going out to hear me or my friends play, or staying home while I go. I wear a wedding band, but a lot of women don't seem to care. If Lee is there she'll angrily glare at those chicks.

58

Winter comes early to Spokane. Lee talks me into going skiing. After I park the car and get out at the ski spot, I look up at the snow covered mountain, with people on a lift being ferried to the top, and say Let me get this shit straight, I'm supposed to lay down some dust to ride that swing to the top of this mother so I can turn around and come back down and go through the whole thing again, if I don't break a leg or worse? I tell her I'll wait at the bar. But she doesn't want to ski without me nor leave me to get drunk in the lodge, so she gets back in the car and never mentions skiing again or makes any attempt to go without me.

59

I wake to a terrible hangover, Lee cowering in a corner. I have no idea why. Last thing I remember is leaving a party. Lee tells me I took her to an after-hours black bordello and left her in the waiting room to go looking for booze. Taken for a hooker by the men coming in, she had to convince them otherwise. After I drank up all our money, on the drive home I turned our argument into one about materialism. To prove how much I despised it, I took some of our clothes and cut them to shreds with her sewing scissors she says, and leads me to a pile of cut-up clothes in the heart of our little living room.

60

When Sandy's mom and stepdad show up at our pad, it's to see me. Lee called them. Vaguely aware they don't drink, I learn they're recovering alcoholics. They talk about their own experiences with blackouts and unacceptable behavior, and leave a book. After they split I compulsively read all of it, in my print junkie way, and identify with a lot, but the next day tell them I'm too young to be an alcoholic. They say alcoholics can stop for a time but not control drinking once they start, so I can prove I'm in control by passing a test: having at least one but not more than five drinks a day for a month.

61

Lee has invited a brother and sister from the local orphanage for Thanksgiving dinner and sends me to the store with money she's saved to make our first holiday memorable. Our rent is forty a month and I only make a hundred, so Lee finds change in our Good Will couch, or saves it from grocery shopping til she gets caught shoplifting so I have to shop. Before I reach the store, a sergeant I know invites me for a beer. After five of them, I call Lee to let her know where I am. She says Remember your deal with Sandy's parents. I say: I got two more to go. Figuring if five drinks proves you can control your drinking, so does seven.

62

Last thing I remember is a bar full of white people, and me arguing with the bartender over Joe McCarthy, who he defends and I curse out before I'm 86'd. Next thing I know I'm coming to in a skid-row, all-night movie theater where bums spend their last quarter to have a place to snooze out of the cold while old Hollywood Westerns play on the screen around the clock. Covered with bruises, blood, and scabs, from a beating or an accident I figure, I search my pockets. All the Thanksgiving money is gone. When I get back to the crib Lee doesn't have to say a thing. I call Sandy's folks. They help generously, including money for Thanksgiving.

63

The first thing I notice is how much clearer everything is. Even the images in my head are sharper, crisper. And music sounds different, as does playing it. And I realize how tacky and tawdry bars can be once they close and the lights come up. Even the people in clubs seem different. I feel sorry for not just the drunks but those who put up with them, or have to, like bartenders and waitresses, and me when I'm playing. I so love not drinking, that at a holiday party when the host hands me the glass of water I asked for and I take a big gulp and taste vodka, I spit it in his face.

64

A lot of the violence in my life ends after I quit drinking, but not in the rest of the world. Malcolm X is shot. The way I figure for his giving up Black Muslim teachings that whites descend from dogs and are devils, after his trip to Mecca where he saw Muslims come in all shades. The death toll in Viet Nam is growing. I can't be sent there, cause the tour is now a year, and I have less than that to go. The war seems more and more suspect to me anyway, especially after Roland shows Lee and me a snapshot of his cousin, a sweet cat before he was drafted, wearing a string of ears he cut off Viet Cong he killed, like a necklace.

65

I'm parking the Pontiac in downtown Spokane when LBJ's speech for the Voting Rights Act comes on the radio. It's hard not to choke up. This big old white Southerner acknowledging the cause Lee's friends have risked their lives in Mississippi for, and she decides to march for, protesting racial discrimination from Bull Connor down South to the versions where we are now. I walk alongside the march to watch over her. Like Charlie and my black brothers back East, I don't participate in mass political acts, just personal ones, like integrating red-neck bars and diners in the segregated South or flaunting my black loves once upon a time.

66

Mad Dog's friend Gary Williams, a country song-writer singer orphaned after his parents died in a car accident, collects objects connected to famous criminals, like a dark-stained stiff old handkerchief dipped in the blood of John Dillinger the night he was shot. Gary lives with an old white-haired lady in a spooky Victorian house where he keeps his collection on the walls of the parlor. He makes a black-and-white film about outlaws of The Great Depression on a sixteen millimeter silent camera and casts me as Baby Face Nelson, fulfilling my fantasy of belonging up there on the silver screen with other movie stars. When Lefty Frizzell comes for a visit with Gary, Lee is thrilled to meet him.

67

Roy, cast as the lead in Moliere's *THE MISER* at Spokane's main theater, convinces the director to see me for the role of Anselme. I've never even heard of Moliere. For the audition I read the part cold, like I read poetry in coffee houses, or MC gigs, including my own. Lee makes my costume out of curtains and stuff she finds in rich folks' trash. On opening night someone asks me if I'm nervous. I say No. But later I can't remember having been on stage. At the party the director praises the actors, and me as an old pro, having fallen for Roy's boasts about my vast experience. But it's a first for me, as I lean against a wall in my shades, pretending I'm way too cool to care.

68

Rabbi ships out, so an older, Irish-American sergeant plays bass with Jimmy and me on a Spokane TV talent contest. When we're hired we're told that the guitar-playing daughter of a local department-store owner is rigged to win. Lee and Linda are in the live audience when Lee snaps at an older lady for saying I look too young to be the band leader. Billed as THE MICHAEL LALLY TRIO we play my version of *SUMMERTIME* juxtaposing Ahmad Jamal phrasing with Nina-Simone-like, piano-length runs and trills. The show is shot on tape and delayed, a brand new technology. When it airs we get to watch it on Linda's and Jimmy's TV.

69

One summer day on the way to Roy and Karen's we hear on the car radio what sounds like a war in the USA. Watts, a neighborhood in L.A., is going up in flames. At their cabin, listening to history unfold, I cite James Baldwin's *THE FIRE NEXT TIME*. We spend my days off hanging out there all summer, swimming in the lake. But when they lay in the sun on the old weathered dock after, I go inside and read, cause my fair Irish skin has been badly burned enough times as a kid. That's how I discover Roy's copy of a new book, *LUNCH POEMS*, which I instantly love for its easy honesty but resent for what I take as its elitist references.

70

I try to get Roy to dig William Saroyan whose books and plays are a comfort to me, and Roy turns me on to Beckett, who I expect to be pretentiously intellectual but turns out more like some of my reticent Irish relatives. When Roy and Karen take us to see Fellini's *8½* I figure I won't understand it. But from the first image it's so accessible to me I leave the theater feeling superior to the man I was when I entered. Like months before when Lee and me went to *A HARD DAY'S NIGHT*. I walked in bugged by the band's impact, as in Brit rock'n'rollers new to Spokane taking jobs from local bands. But I walked out after it wanting to be a Beatle.

71

After giving up drinking, smoking pot seems more potent, especially listening to rare tapes of Lenny Bruce and Lord Buckley that Wilson gets hold of. I don't try LSD, yet, the newest kick on the scene, and peyote makes me sick. But when I discover the chord changes in a Beatles tune are close to ones I use in my jazz improvisations, I add it to my act: *Listen, do you wanna know a secret, ooh wah ooh.* When Dylan goes electric, the local radio station plays *SUBTERRANEAN HOMESICK BLUES* over and over but pronounces his name Dial-in. Rock'n'roll begins replacing jazz at a lot of the Spokane clubs we've been playing in.

72

When Thornton Bell shows up, a sax playing enlisted man still in his teens with a winning smile in a dark handsome face and most of his musical history from his native Georgia, I ask him over to jam with Jimmy and me and our new bass player. Thorn blows us away. We play a few gigs as a quartet where he cooks, and we try to keep up. One night after a gig we go to a black club where an electric-piano-playing old black dude holds sway as king of the local jazz scene. Bell asks to sit in and blows the old man away. The club owner hires Bell and us to replace the old cat's band. But Bell soon replaces the bass player and me, keeping only Jimmy.

73

Lee is sure I'm cheating on her. I'm not. She accuses me of having sex with Kat. We never even kissed. And with the blonde upstairs I don't even find attractive. One day I come back from work to find Lee up there with the blonde. Turns out her handsome Air Policeman husband has disappeared, leaving her with their little girl. Through sobs and tears she reveals he's been having an affair. It takes her a while to admit, not with another woman but with another handsome Air Policeman. When it was discovered, they were discharged and took off for California, leaving the blonde and the little girl behind.

74

Hugh and his lady get married in the nude in a ceremony on Mount Rainier and move to Oregon. When we camp with Karen and Roy overnight on Rainer, I sleep in the car. Roy's student loan gets him a boat in Seattle, first time I sleep on one. He sells it when he gets into The Iowa Writers Workshop. Kat and Val follow him there. Sandy gets out of jail before Billy. When he does, they break up. She'll later change her name to Sharma and become a sex guru. Jimmy and Linda split for England where he's been transferred. Bill Tandy takes off for Santa Rosa, California, after marrying his underage bride with her parents' blessing.

75

Before Wilson leaves for law school in Berkeley,
he and Ramona visit our basement pad with her
mother, daughter of the last Colville tribal chief
and the only royalty I've ever been that close to.
She sits on our Good Will couch, perfectly straight
backed and regal. She speaks American English,
as I always call it, haltingly and seriously, her
accent unique and melodic. I assume her original
language is that of her tribe. She treats us with
such graciousness, I fall in love with her. A few
years later, on Thanksgiving, of all tragic ironies,
she and whoever is driving, was it one of her
children or someone else in the family? are killed
in a head-on collision with a drunken white man.

76

John Sinclair, editor of a Detroit little mag, rejects
some poems I submit but writes: *Who are you?*
I reply angrily *I'm the writing you rejected.* After
seeing a notice in *THE VILLAGE VOICE* for a new
mag, *KALEIDOSCOPE*, I send work and get a note
from the editor that my writing moved her deeply,
and a twenty-five-dollar check for a story and some
poems. First money I've ever made from writing,
after years of rejections. Lee says She thinks you're
the old man in your story. So I write back *I'm 23,
married and about to get out of the Air Force.* She
offers me a job at the mag and a pad in Brooklyn
Heights to live in, along with her patronage while
I write what she calls *The Great American Novel.*

77

At the base to get my discharge papers, I'm stopped by a Captain I don't know, objecting to the length of my hair. He orders me to get it cut by the numbers, meaning according to regulations, and report back to him. I say I'm on my way to pick up my discharge papers. If you want to get out, he snarls, better not disobey my order. I get my hair cut, report back to him and am legal to leave. I swear never to get my hair cut again til I feel like it. We pack what fits into the trunk, backseat, and part of the front seat of the Pontiac: paintings, records, books, and clothes, with just enough room on the front seat for Lee to squeeze in beside me.

78

We stop at Crater Lake to see Hugh, then San Francisco where everything is changing except City Lights, drive from Laramie to Cheyenne in a blizzard at night with no dashboard lights and two flat tires, visit Roy and Karen in Iowa City and see Nelson Algren and Kurt Vonnegut. In New York state, a deer suddenly appears, I miss it with the front of the car but clip it with the rear. Getting out to see how badly it's hurt we watch it stand up shakily and, still wobbling, stumble into the woods. We visit Lee's parents, then her grandparents' farm, and stop at Saint Bonaventure's to revisit where we first met, the campus and school buildings so much smaller than we remember.

THE BROOKLYN HEIGHTS & SOUTH ORANGE PART TWO SONNETS

"The reality that I had known no longer existed."

—Marcel Proust

1

Rita, the editor of *KALEIDOSCOPE*, a tall shapely redhead, is waiting for us outside an elegant old townhouse on Remson Street with the publisher, a dark-haired goateed guy, half her size, who makes tons of money as a consultant for corporations and the government on computers, those room-size machines. It keeps him out of town for months, which is why he lets us use his pad full of priceless antiques, including a collection of frog art: statuettes and exotic carvings from around the world that, he shows me, if turned over display enormous penises. I haven't shaved since Spokane so I have a bit of a beard too.

2

After the publisher splits, Rita goes for sandwiches while Lee and I unpack the car, carting the first load into the museum of an apartment. I come right back out to find the car broken into. They only got my jazzman vines, but that's where I hid my discharge money. Luckily Lee had talked me into converting it to travelers checks. Rita returns to find Lee sobbing and shaking as if she herself was violated. While we leave her inside to calm down, Rita helps me get the rest from the car where she asks Is Lee always this neurotic? Later I go to Jersey to sell the Pontiac to my next-door cousin-the-cop's father-in-law and visit my ailing mother.

3

For twelve weeks I carry manuscripts and galleys daily, by foot, from midtown Manhattan to the printer on Canal Street. The magazine, on loose narrow pages, comes curled in a kaleidoscope tube with tiny samples from Village artisans and stores. I run into Curtis Powell, just back from Europe, in the post office near Cooper Union, visit DeWitt, Mel, and Cliff. Cal and Cissie, and Lynn and Teddy, visit us in our plush pad. I get to know Izzy Young at his new FOLKLORE CENTER above OBIES, where I hear him ask a teenager what Andy Warhol's appeal is, after a monotone Warhol radio interview. The kid says He's cool. Izzy points at me, says He's cool, Warhol's cold.

4

When *NEW YORK TIMES* theater critic, Walter Kerr, writes of a lack of young playwrights, I call *THE TIMES*, ask for him, and am put right through. I tell him You're wrong, I'm a young playwright, can you help me? He says he isn't allowed to, but will send me a list of producers. The closest I get to any is when, from behind a door with one of those eyeholes, an older woman claims the lady I'm looking for has gone away. She asks what I want anyway. I tell her I have a play. She says Oh dear I just can't do any more, I mean SHE isn't doing any more plays. Neither of us says anything for a minute. Finally she says I'm really sorry young man, I wish I could help you.

5

My old man blames my beard for the downturn in my mom's condition, as he blamed my past behavior for her heart attacks. When I visit, little kids in my old neighborhood point at my beard and yell BEATNIK! After an operation at Saint Michael's, the doc claims he removed all ma's cancer. But when she has a heart attack in the recovery room, a callous nurse tells us to get her stuff out of her hospital room. My sister Joan asks Why? The nurse says Because she isn't coming back and we need the room. At first we think she means our ma's going home. Then the surgeon says he actually didn't get all the cancer out so death from heart failure is best.

6

My brother Buddy, who already had a few too many, has trouble with the pay phone trying to call his wife, so rips it off the wall. We all take turns sitting with ma. I'm alone with her when she suddenly calls out for her oldest, the friar still in Japan, and her youngest: me. I say I'm here ma, it's Michael. She opens her eyes to stare at me with so much fear I want to disappear. I think: She sees death approaching. But also think She doesn't recognize me cause of this fucking beard. I'm holding her hand as the line on the heart monitor goes flat. Back at the house Joan reads a note ma wrote in the hospital with instructions on caring for daddy.

7

While my siblings comfort our father, I shave,
marveling at how soft the beardless skin feels,
like a baby's. He thanks me, thinking I did it
so he won't be embarrassed at the wake. But I
made a secret vow to my ma to never grow a
beard again. Before the wake starts, he has us
look at her body, saying This is not your mother,
she's in heaven. Then has me and my sisters steer
away aunts who might start keening. There's the
usual lighthearted bantering we do at funerals,
with old men pulling secret pints from pockets
or doing magic coin tricks for the smaller kids,
everyone sharing stories of ma that brings tears
to all our eyes, that and all the cigarette smoke.

8

Our old man doesn't want the wake to go on
for days so my brother Robert, the cop, calls
the new pastor to ask that the funeral Mass be
the next day. He says neither he nor his priests
are able to do it then. Robert says that's ok cause
the archbishop of our diocese and the president
of Seton Hall, the local Catholic college, a mon-
signor, plan to say a High Mass for the funeral
with top Franciscans from Thirty-First Street, as
we all call Saint Francis church in Manhattan
where our oldest brother started his priestly
career. Other Franciscans will be coming too,
since our big brother's in Japan and can't make
the funeral. The pastor finds a way to be there.

9

The after-the-funeral party goes on for days, as they always do. When I ask why we Irish do that, my next-door Aunt Mary says So the family can get used to their loss before they're left alone. The first thing my siblings and me have to deal with is what to do about our father. At sixty-seven, he's already had one heart attack, has developed diabetes, and will now need domestic help. Like most men, he doesn't cook or care for a home's insides other than repairs. But he doesn't want to move in with my siblings, who all have homes of their own. So, since Lee and me are apartment sitting, it's agreed we should move in with him. I resist. Lee doesn't, wanting me away from Rita.

10

Lee is sure Rita and me are having an affair. I never even kissed her, or anyone else since we got married. Lee doesn't believe that. Then one day we come back to the Brooklyn Heights crib to find Rita's panties hanging in the bathroom. Lee can't accept her explanation: she was in the neighborhood and unexpectedly got her period and, since she has a key, let herself in to wash out her panties and then leave them to dry. Lee asks Why didn't she bring the wet panties home with her? Then Rita responds to my ramblingly abstract novel by suggesting I throw it out and start over. I refuse. Her patronage ends.

11

My old man moves into the first floor bedroom he built for my late crippled grandma. We take my parents' room, most nights falling out of bed laughing, reading to each other from William Goldman's *TEMPLE OF GOLD* or Lennon's *IN HIS OWN WRITE*. Ma was my old man's secretary so typed and made carbons of her newsy letters to her older kids, including her reports of my troubles over the years. Joan, a secretary too, retypes them, removing any bad news about me, then destroys the originals. But even censored, I can see my mother was a fine writer. My seventh-grade drop-out father wrote rhyming poems to customers every Christmas.

12

My sister Irene's wedding, planned for after ma's operation, now happens without her, the reception held around the corner in our big sister Joan's backyard, a little patch of grass with a blanket-sized vegetable garden. Irene's husband's family are all German-born and proper. Our Aunt Peggy and Uncle Lydic display the kind of Irish party behavior that endears them to me, but not to the Germans. Uncle Lydie sings beautifully but then makes a few Nazi jokes with *sieg heil* salutes, while Aunt Peggy does cartwheels in her best dress to show the little kids she still can, and in the process shows us all her undergarments.

13

Cal visits and decides he wants to move his family to Jersey. Roy and Karen convince us to take a bus trip to Portland, Maine, where Dick Harvey takes us to the blessing of the boats of Portuguese lobstermen, then the film of *WHO'S AFRAID OF VIRGINIA WOOLF?* We discuss it for days. With my discharge money, I buy an old Mercury to drive us back in, stopping in Provincetown, where Lee and Karen notice men eyeing my tight pants. Lee tells us how she once slept on the beach there and a very drunk Kerouac stumbled over her in the night, cursing her for being on HIS beach. We go swimming, and I let them talk me into lying on the sand with them in the summer sun.

14

By nightfall, shivering with fever, my skin starting to blister, I lie on the back seat of the Merc, the others up front, Roy or Karen driving, me in and out of feverish sleep. They bring me food when they stop, and leave me in the car when we cross a stretch of water by ferry. I can't pull my Beatle boots on, or move without excruciating pain. After it subsides, back in the city we see underground flicks in a basement: *HALLELUJAH THE HILLS* with future friend Taylor Mead, John Cassavete's *SHADOWS*, Michael Roemer's *NOTHING BUT A MAN*, and more. I sell Roy the Merc to drive back to Iowa City.

15

While I was away in the service, Spanish Harry got a degree in psychology and now works at Overbrook mental hospital, made famous in jazz circles by a James Moody composition he wrote while incarcerated there for a heroin habit: *LAST TRAIN FROM OVERBROOK*. One of my old man's political cronies gets me a job there as assistant recreational therapist. Two thousand a year to spend time on a baseball field with the patients, or on rainy days in a dank, dusty wire cage called a rec room in one building's moldy basement, where the recreation consists of an uneven ping pong table and a lot of soiled, outdated magazines with half their pages ripped out.

16

My first day at Overbrook a patient yells my name. It's a kid younger than me from my neighborhood. When I ask why he's here he tells me he hot-wired a car for joy riding, which he's notorious for, and when the cops chased him, crashed it. They roughed him up for that and booked him for auto theft and, to justify their getting physical: resisting arrest. When they got the police doctor to treat him, the doc lectured my friend about God and sin. He told the doc he didn't believe in God. So the doc wrote him up for psychiatric treatment. The cops took him to Overbrook where I run into him two years later. His file confirms this.

17

Lee has a paperback by a man named Robert Lowry the nuns at her high school confused with Robert Lowell so invited him to speak. When he read from his self-published novel, *THE PRINCE OF PRIDE STARRING*, the nuns were shocked, but not quick enough to stop Lee from buying a signed copy. The book's narrator is a man distraught from the death of his child, and his wife leaving him over it. When stopped by a cop for speeding, he's taken to the station, but his distress gets him transferred to a mental institution: Lee's big fear after being committed once, before we wed, for cutting her wrists with a razor blade.

18

Lee turned me on to the movie *DAVID AND LISA*. I turned her on to the novel *ONE FLEW OVER THE CUCKOO'S NEST*. Now I'm working in a place that isn't a fictional creation. The head recreational therapist, my boss, a shaven-headed old man, had been a champion wrestler in his day and still has a powerful physique. He likes to point out the framed photos of himself as a young wrestler on his office wall, a room as dank and grimy as the patients' quarters, with the same dark stained walls and institutional odor that seem like weapons of depression, intended to bring the spirit down. But none of that bothers him.

19

Sometimes on sunny days my boss brings a medicine ball out to toss around with patients. He gets a big kick out of throwing it so hard it knocks them down. Most are so drugged they have no reflexes anyway. There are few psychiatrists for the high number of patients. If lucky, a patient sees a doctor every few months. The attendants caring for patients are underpaid, only a thousand a year, and mostly undereducated, young, black men. If a patient displays rebelliousness or independence the attendants request an increase in their meds, and the docs always acquiesce. Most of the patients sit or shuffle around in a semi-stupor.

20

One bright, articulate, black woman patient is a jazz musician once married to a famous piano player, I learn. We talk of Lady Day and others we admire, and Manhattan jazz joints we know. I ask her why she's in here, she seems so normal except for a heavy sadness. She says she experienced the trauma of losing someone in horrendous circumstances and had a breakdown that got her put into Overbrook. Later I ask an attendant why she hasn't been discharged by now. He tells me to mind my own business. Next time we pick up the patients on her ward, she isn't there. I'm told she flipped out so was put in solitary.

21

In men's solitary my boss opens the little window
to look in through the thick metal door of a cell
and begins taunting a well-known black athlete
til he charges the door. I instinctively step back,
as though he could crash through it and grab me.
My boss laughs, as the man pounds the door. At
my first patient baseball game the black athlete
is allowed to play. My boss has me umpire from
behind the pitcher and be sure to call a strike if I
see one. When I call a strike on the black athlete
he comes after me with the bat. My boss laughs
as the man chases me around for a while til they
throw a net over him, take the bat away, and put a
straight jacket on him to take him back to his cell.

22

We're on the baseball field with the usual half
aware patients when a car parks nearby, the driver
a hefty, dolled-up, middle-aged woman, mother
of a lanky teenage white boy who, after his father
abandoned them, woke her from a nap coming at
her with an electric drill. She escaped. He was
locked up at Overbrook. My boss lets him visit
her in her car, calling my attention to their kiss-
ing like lovers before she shoves his head into
her big bosom, while the kid squirms in what
looks like delight. I can't see what his hands
are doing. My boss calmly explains that the kid
deserves release from his teenage sexual tension
and his poor mother doesn't have anyone but him.

23

When I find out some night shift attendants
force patients to have sex with them, I call
it to the attention of the administration. They
don't seem surprised or anxious to do much
about it, treating it like it's compensation for
the attendants' low pay. In an old Victorian
house on the grounds, where they keep teenage
patients, I befriend a bright girl brought in
after freaking out at The Beatles' Shea Stadium
concert. She seems more reasonable and calm
than most of the staff, but they won't let her go.
I identify more and more with the patients and
not with the other attendants, but I have no control over any of it. Neither does Spanish Harry.

24

When we saw *A SHOT IN THE DARK* back in
Spokane, Lee laughed so loud we missed half
the lines and had to see it again. She isn't
laughing at all as summer comes to an end. Nor
am I, fearing I'll be locked up in Overbrook
too, after I learn other workers there have been.
Lee's restless under my old man's constant
surveillance and sarcastic remarks about her
shorts being too short or her jeans painted on.
And my whole family seems suspicious of her
not being pregnant after two years of marriage.
So when Roy writes us to join him in Iowa City
insisting that I'm a better writer than the students
in the Writers Workshop there, we decide to go.

THE IOWA CITY SONNETS

"Live ignorance rots us worse than any grave."

—Philip Whelan

1

Our first night in Iowa we sleep on Roy and
Karen's floor. Next day at the registrar's, I
tell them I'm here for the Writers Workshop.
The lady asks if my application has been
accepted. I say I'm here to apply now. She
says It's too late. I tell her I'm a married vet,
after four years in the military I just want to
be a part of the famous Iowa Writers Workshop.
She asks where I got my B.A. from. I tell her
I don't have one. She explains I have to have
a B.A. and my writing accepted, but takes pity
on me and fast tracks an application for the
undergraduate Writers Workshop. I'm accepted
under The G.I. Bill the day before classes start.

2

We move off Roy and Karen's floor to our
second basement-apartment-in-an-old-house-
owned-by-an-old-farm-couple. Across the river
from campus, the only daylight comes from
two little eyebrow windows looking out on the
cement steps leading down to it; Karen, Roy,
Kat, and Val the first to descend. Val not only
followed Roy to Iowa but to film classes, both
now convinced it's the art form of our time.
They all live outside Iowa City in rented farm
houses, just as they had in Washington state.
But instead of raising chickens, Val now raises
mosquitoes in a huge mason jar, observing their
cycle of birth, life, and death, with deep interest.

3

I tap the shoulder of a teenager sitting in front of me in one of my classes, to ask what the instructor just said. She turns to me, gives a little laugh, and replies: I have noo ideeeaa. In what I soon discover is a kind of Midwestern drawl peculiar to Iowans. She's Suzanne Burgess from Cedar Rapids, with a uniquely pretty, porcelain-doll-like face, who finds almost everything amusing. Learning who my wife is, she describes first noticing Lee crossing the foot bridge over The Iowa River in one of her distinct homemade outfits, flowing black cape billowing behind her from the wind and her determined pace.

4

After a D on a Henry James test I wait in the hall for the professor. As he passes, I ask if he has a minute. He tries to hurry by, saying he's busy, but I put one hand on the wall in front of him and another behind, so he has nowhere to go unless he wants to get into a wrestling match. I tell him I'm twenty-four, a published writer who's read all of James's books, some twice, yet got a D on a test kids who only read Cliff Notes got B's on. So he checks my bluebook and says I need to show him I'm paying attention by giving him back what he's taught before going into my own theories about James being a humorist at heart.

5

In a class on modern poetry, I write a paper for a tall, shy, not-too-much-older than me, Larry Kramer, who notes on it *You have one of the strangest prose styles I've ever read.* So, unasked, I do another for extra credit, in which I analyze the structure of Ezra Pound's haiku-like *IN A STATION OF THE METRO*, using only rhymed, iambic-pentameter quatrains. Including two lines rhyming poem with the tome in epitome, which I pronounce epi-tome, til Kramer corrects me. He seems bewildered by it and admits he has no idea how to grade it.

6

Val puts me in his first student film, the only person in a silent short about a prisoner who doesn't realize his cell's unlocked. When he does, he hesitates to leave the familiarity of it. Val says it's about the existential dilemma. Karen reproduces photos from *RAMPARTS* of burned and mutilated Vietnamese kids, blows them up and glues them to a sandwich board, writes *NAPALM OUR AUSCHWITZ* on it and walks around Iowa City. People stop to ask What's napalm? Roy does a leaflet on what it is and how our military uses it. Some people curse at Karen, or spit on her, or grab the leaflets from her to tear up, or throw in the gutter.

7

When Lee marches in an anti-war protest,
I keep an eye on her from the crowd of pro-
war onlookers. One coed marcher holds a sign
MAKE LOVE NOT WAR, and a young guy
watching from the pro-war crowd screams
WHORE! I knock into him, hard, pretending
it's an accident. He backs off. Some in the
pro-war crowd begin to chant: KILL! KILL!
KILL! A weasely white guy weaving among
the crowd urges them to throw rocks at the
marchers. I hustle Lee away. At the rally later
Karen and Roy's mentor, Doctor Barnet,
pompously lectures the crowd as its superior,
using Marxist terminology I find off-putting.

8

I wear the inexpensive suit bought for my
sister Irene's wedding to campus plays like
UBU ROI where I first encounter Ray Di-
Palma's unique stage presence, and later
others, like John Getz, or Mary Beth Sup-
pinger, future Hurt, from Marshalltown, Iowa,
Jean Seberg's hometown. And when Michael
Dennis Browne, assistant prof in The Poetry
Workshop, includes me in a reading to raise
funds for wounded Vietnamese kids, with
famous writers like Vance Bourjaily and
Kurt Vonnegut. The first time I read poetry
in a school, let alone a university, and not
a bar or coffee house or on the street drunk.

9

The G.I. Bill helps with tuition, not rent or food, so even after Lee gets a job as a telephone operator I work for extra bread on the houses of professors, doing minor repairs like in my old man's business growing up. We can't afford to rent a piano, so between classes and odd jobs I drop by the music room in the student union to play. One day a young white sax player joins me and we jam. He suggests we start a band. He's a nice guy and I dig his playing, so say sure, but later think it over and decide to quit playing music gigs to focus on my writing, when not in class, or working extra jobs.

10

In a review of *NOTHING BUT A MAN* in *THE DAILY IOWAN*, grad-student playwright star, Nicholas Meyer, calls Abbey Lincoln *A beautiful, yet unglamorous newcomer*. I write to the editor that *Meyer is obviously the newcomer*. Pointing out that Lincoln was in her first film in 1957 and has been singing and acting professionally since the 1940s. *So Meyer should have said Lincoln was a newcomer to him*. A lot of professors and grad students come off as smug about their supposed superior knowledge which makes me want to correct them.

11

On a sunny Fall afternoon, walking down the main street of Iowa City eating popsicles, me still holding the wrapper in my free hand, a Chevy double parks and a teenager gets out and punches me in the face. I rock back on the flamenco heels of my Beatle boots, still holding the wrapper and popsicle, the kid surprised I'm still standing. Dropping the popsicle and wrapper, I throw him onto the hood of a parked car. A second young man runs from the Chevy to jump on my back and start hitting me, yelling Leave my li'l brother alone! I yell Your little brother just punched me in the face for no reason motherfucker!

12

Lee screams for help. People keep walking. The driver, a grown man, emerges and signals the others to get back in the Chevy, then drives off just as a cop finally responds to Lee's pleas. She points at the car leaving, but the cop doesn't even look. When she tells him I was attacked by two young guys for no reason, I add They looked like farm boys, not students or townies. He says What do you expect with hair like that? And walks away. Our style and my hair, longer than most men's, has become a provocation. A few nights later at an anti-war event Roy and Karen invite us to, I'm pointed out as some kind of hero with my now yellowing black eye.

13

My Undergraduate Poetry Workshop teacher,
James Tate, a grad student younger than me
who just won The Yale Younger Poets Award
comes across as a world weary, sardonic, old
man, despite his youth. He tells me You won't
win any prizes. And says my style is too raw
and inconsistent for editors and publishers
and poetry contest judges. I'm one of the few
students of his who's had poems published.
Like Nathan Whiting, who convinces me to
join the class and Tate to let me in. Nathan
is my real teacher, an original in every way,
including not showing up for finals in courses
we share, explaining he's just there to learn.

14

Nathan gets me to re-write. Something I always
resisted, assuming the words come from God, or
some muse or angel or the voices of my ances-
tors, somewhere beyond my comprehension
and control. I figure I shouldn't mess with that
source by correcting it, til Nathan. He's softly
suggestive in ways I can hear. I admire him for
that, and for spending every day writing poetry.
And for running everywhere, for fun or to get
around, like no other adult does, yet. And for the
longest hair I've seen on a man. Others have let
theirs grow, a la the Brit bands, but not as long as
his, down to his shoulders, as thin and wispy as
his chin beard, like a paler, blonder Chinese sage.

15

The phone company is in a windowless fortress on the other side of Iowa City where I meet Lee to walk her home when she gets off work at midnight. I usually get there with time to spare. One winter night, with snow falling lightly on the foot, or so, already on the ground, no person, or car, or movement on the street, I watch steam from my breath make tiny clouds. And in that muffled silence snow creates, can hear the drumming in my ears. Suddenly I get that I'm standing on the surface of a small planet slowly spinning through the darkness of the universe, just a little ball of rock with this tiny creature clinging to it by the force of a gravity I've been taking for granted way too long.

16

On a spring day I show up at SOAPBOX SOUND OFF, the Campus venue for political discourse, to hear Roy and Karen speak out against the war. In the crowd I notice the guy from that first anti-war march in the Fall who encouraged the pro-war crowd to throw rocks at the peaceniks. When Roy and Karen finish speaking, he steps up to the microphone to attack them as unpatriotic, unAmerican traitors. He's speaking as head of the campus Young Americans for Freedom. He pisses me off so much, when he's done I jump up on the platform and find myself in front of the microphone before I even realize I made the move.

17

I'm used to microphones, but not spontaneous political expression. People shout LOUDER! I speak up, about my being a married, tax paying veteran, who's voted in every election since turning twenty-one, four years ago. Most in the crowd of students have never been out of school, or in the military, or paid taxes, or voted. Including the Young Americans for Freedom guy. I say I served in the military to defend all of our rights, like the right to freedom of speech, including opposing our government's policies, if we feel like it. I step down to a burst of applause and someone asking me to speak at an anti-war rally in Des Moines in a few weeks.

18

When I pick Lee up after her day shift, she's angry and shaken, demanding to know what I did. She says she put through a long distance call from the head of campus security to the FBI headquarters in Omaha and stayed on the line to make sure of the connection. Though I know she and the other operators listen in out of boredom. What she heard was a list of names, including mine. I tell her I stood up for Roy and Karen at Soapbox Sound Off. She's scared cause I'm now on an FBI list. I'm mad at the campus cops and FBI for nosing around in a student free speech forum and adding my name to a government file. I didn't want to join anything before but do now.

19

The first demonstration I take part in is at the post office, the only federal building in Iowa City, in support of a local guy on active duty in the Air Force who is being courtmartialed for taking part in an anti-war protest. I meet another student vet there and we decide to start a campus VETERANS AGAINST THE WAR group. Then we travel to Chicago to create, with WWII, Korean, and other Cold War vets, a U.S. VETERANS AGAINST THE VIETNAM WAR group. No Viet Nam War veterans. Yet. We take part in antiwar protests all over the Midwest.

20

On a sunny Spring day I speak from a stage on the steps of the capitol in Des Moines, after an anti-war march. Most of the speakers refer to the crowd as You. Or don't refer to them at all, as if talking to themselves, or each other. When I get up to talk with nothing prepared, I say We instead of You, and talk about being a veteran from a family of cops, and how I thought it was My country right or wrong but now know it's My country right or wrong, if right I'll fight to defend it, if wrong I'll fight to change it. As I riff on what I'm learning about all the lies used to justify the war in Viet Nam, it feels like jazz but improvising with words instead of notes.

21

With Roy, Karen, and the artists John and Joan Hanor, we go to see a sculpture show at The Chicago Art Institute. My first time in a museum. All the art I've seen has been in books or poster reproductions. I dig the Louises: Nevelson and Bourgeois. But just outside the exhibit room I keep circling scratched stainless steel boxes balancing precariously, in reality welded together. I labored for my father, now myself, hammering and soldering, working with glass, metal, wood and wire, miter boxes, saws, vice grips, hand drills, and the rest, all the time calling myself a poet, a musician, an artist. All that is evoked by my first encounter with a David Smith sculpture.

22

During a break from summer semester we fly to Jersey where parts of Newark are in flames, like where I'd seen Daddy Grace's purple-robed nuns break open a fire hydrant to baptize sinners, and Grace in his ermine robe on a throne in his church, now burned up like Father Divine's Peace restaurant and the nearby home of a black girl I dated and the bars we hung in. On the cover of *LIFE* a photo of a little black boy in a puddle of blood shot by a cop for looting the six pack of soda beside him. Arguing with my cop brother-in-law, at one point he yells I'd shoot my own father if he was looting, and if I wasn't married to your sister I'd take out my gun and shoot YOU.

23

W. S. Merwin comes to Iowa to read, introduced by Marvin Bell as The Prince of Poetry. Later, talking with him on a back porch, a joint passes in an empty toilet-paper-roll makeshift pipe. I decline, my street experience making me suspicious of toking in public. Workshop poet Slater notices. We met through Lee. After he spied her in an outfit he had to cross the street to compliment, they became good friends. I dig his pretty little brown-skinned wife. He's a tall, thin, white Iowan with hay-colored hair who talks old-style hip city slang. Raised by grandparents, he slept on their couch as a kid discovering The Blues on the radio and deciding he was a White Negro.

24

There are bars and bars in Iowa City, full of college cliques and gossip, Workshop writers at Kenney's, where on the men's room graffiti-filled wall someone scrawled *MICHAEL LALLY IS COOL*. Meant ironically, I'm certain, since a lot of grad students wield irony like a weapon. But people I trust assure me it's not, and that the same thing is also written on the ladies room wall. Tough little New Yorker Jane DeLynn, on acid she says, asks if I'm fucking the mysterious Alice Notley who I walked home once. I tell her I don't cheat on my wife.

25

Waking to what sounds like tiny feet scurrying,
I think Mice. Or worse: Rats. As Lee hides under
the covers, I sit up in the dark to pull the cord
on the naked light bulb hanging over our bed
and feel something stir the air around my face as it
flutters by. A bat! I run to the closet for my skinny
brim, pull it down to cover my hair, grab our broom
and swing. The air merely displaces around the
bat. But I keep at it till I wear the bat out and
it flops to the cement floor, its little face like all
the bats in old Dracula movies. I get the broom
on top of it, get the door open, and then sweep
it out into the night. The landlord gives us a bad-
minton racket that works when the bat returns.

26

After three bat visits, we move to Moffets, aka
Cockroach Arms. You enter from either of two
perpendicular streets. From one, you climb to
a second floor hallway lined with screen doors,
the solid doors behind them usually open so you
can see into each crib. On the other you enter a
first floor hallway. They meet at a staircase, an
Escher drawing come to life, with a cacophonous
soundtrack mixing stereo music from each pad.
We're on the second floor facing the steps to the
first. Galley kitchen, living room windows look
out on downtown Iowa City rooftops, bedroom
with tiny skylight in black ceiling and star decals
that glow so it's like sleeping under a night sky.

27

Our first Sunday morning I hear scratching on our screen door and find a bag of jelly donuts and Danishes outside it, like my old man brought home for us kids after Mass on Sunday mornings. I figure whoever left them comes from the same tradition. While we eat them, he returns to introduce himself: actor and Workshop poet Ray DiPalma, Italian-American from outside Pittsburgh who loves books as much as I do. His pad, at the bottom of the steps outside our door, spans the two floors where they join, like a big elevator shaft with a loft bed. We're neighborhood guys among Ivy League alums, like his friend David Milch, grad-student playwright star from Yale.

28

Dropping by the music room to satisfy the urge I find grad-student poet Ralph Dickey at the piano. A sweet cat with an unpretentious vibe and beautiful copper-toned skin, he has good hands with a Bill Evans influence. A better technician than me, he says I swing in a way he wishes he could. We're instant friends. He tells me his mother is white, his absent father black. Raised his first seven years in a white suburb, when a white step-dad entered his life he was taken to a black aunt's home to live in the Detroit ghetto, an interloper in both scenes getting shit for it from all sides. Now he dates a white coed who hides it from her parents.

29

THE PAPER PLACE, devoted entirely to paperbacks, has stacks of their biggest seller: *TROUT FISHING IN AMERICA* by Richard Brautigan. Harry James Epstein sits behind the raised counter at the front of the store, like a caricature of a tiny judge in some wacky Warner Brothers cartoon. Or his brother Glen Miller Epstein, a bit taller than Harry, sporting an early-Beatles, mop-top look, bangs and all, and a cat-that-ate-the-mouse grin usually on his boyish face. Harry is little-boy height with an unruly mass of curls atop his anything-but-boyish face with its permanent leer, his pad famous for orgiastic stoned parties and white fridge he hand lettered an entire short story on.

30

THE PAPER PLACE is owned by Gerry, who lives above it with a dark-haired beauty of Irish descent. She left her husband for him, a man twice her age with the face of an old pub fixture, the hack of a chain smoker, who stays half bagged on wine but speaks eloquently and knows a lot about books, which in a college town can be very seductive. One sunny day a passerby spies Gerry crawling from the doorway, bleeding badly. The beauty's husband had stabbed him. After months in hospital, Gerry walks around with one arm in a wire device, like a little sculpture emerging from his body, bent arm stuck out as if he's about to extend his hand and bow to his partner in a minuet.

31

Lee's belly gets too big for Ma Bell. I need more work. Someone hips me to a part-time gig at the Proctor & Gamble plant. Up at 5AM for a bus as far as it goes, I hitch or walk a mile to P&G where truckers pay me to load or unload their rigs till I leave for class, or to meet *DECEMBER* mag's Curt Johnson who comes to visit. A tall lanky older man, he dismisses my Workshop teachers as bores. Or a shapely little New York Jewish bird with long dark tresses, who invites me to her crib and I go. But when she throws her arms around my neck to kiss me passionately, I realize I can't cheat on Lee. The coed seems to find it pitiable that I don't have the good sense to take advantage of what she's offered.

32

I help radicalize Ken W, a big Iowa farm boy who becomes my political partner. After one anti-war protest, Lee repairs a rip in his pants, then steps into one leg and pulls it up past her waist, his thigh bigger around than her hips, which is why he's on a football scholarship he loses after being radicalized and writing an expose of the football program as big business, where young athletes are injected with drugs when badly injured so they can keep playing without feeling pain, often causing permanent damage, and scholarships are supplemented with illegal monetary rewards, all to keep the teams viable and the alumni money pouring in.

33

Ken and me are buying ice cream cones when a guy I know says Hi. After he splits Ken asks What IS he? I tell him A grad student from New York. But he keeps asking. I finally get it and say He's Italian. To Ken, Iowa City is urban life. His size and strength are helpful when we travel to anti-war protests all over the Midwest and beyond. I keep an eye on the edge of the crowd for impending police action and Ken gets us out when I give him the signal. Like a night in Ann Arbor at a police station protesting earlier arrests. As the cops attack our explosion of adrenalin, emotion, solidarity, and youthful exuberance in the face of aggression, I cue Ken to get us out just in time.

34

When Lee and I meet with the Catholic chaplain to discuss our unborn baby's Baptism, we walk in on him and Muhammad Ali and get to shake Ali's big powerful hand and see his handsome face up close. He's calmer and more humble than on TV. And taller. The chaplain is a friend of his from some mutual experience in the past neither reveal. We figure he scheduled our meeting so we'd witness his friendship with the greatest boxer of our time, and icon of resistance to the war he's been stripped of his title and the right to defend it for refusing to fight in. Ali explains in a speech in a campus hall later that evening: No Viet Cong ever called me nigger.

35

Before Karen and Roy leave to film revolutions
in Africa, they're sprayed in the face with mace
by campus cops, handcuffed, and arrested for pro-
testing recruiters for Dow, the corporation making
the napalm the U.S. is dropping on the Vietnamese,
a flaming petroleum jelly that sticks to clothes and
skin. I publicly debate City Manager Frank Smiley
over the protestors' rights, and at the next protest
join a crowd trying to keep students from a Marine
recruiter by blocking an entrance nonviolently, a
gang of raging jocks insulting and punching us.
I'm happy to see student writer Denis Johnson
among us, til a jock climbs to the metal awning
we're under and begins stomping on our heads.

36

When the police arrive, they arrest the pro-
testors, not the jocks attacking them. I slip
away to watch from the sidelines. As the last
protestor is taken away, George Starbuck,
head of The Writers Workshop, steps from
the spectators to join them. Impressed, I do
too. We know the school can't expel the pro-
testors now without firing him. In the holding
cell we're fed bland baloney sandwiches as
a lawyer advises we plead *Nolo Contendere.*
I urge pleading innocent. The judge lectures
us before asking how we plead. Everyone says
Nolo Contendere. I say Not guilty. They're
each fined fifty bills. My case is dismissed.

37

Outside court, a TV reporter shoots questions at me. I answer thoughtfully. Then Lee Weingrad makes a joke from the crowd and I laugh. Watching the news that night on our neighbors the Suttons' TV, when the reporter asks me a serious question, they cut to me laughing, as though in response. My first experience with biased TV news editing. Weingrad, a tall, funny, smart, Jewish guy from New York, talks me into running for the student senate as the married students representative, part of his plan for us to take over that body. We get everyone we know to pack my first session. When I make a motion to do away with *In Loco Parentis*, the paternalistic rules that control all students, the crowd erupts.

38

I use *ROBERT'S RULES* to confuse the fraternity boys who run the student governing body till we've voted to put students in charge of fees, dormitories, and their own governance. Newspapers across the Midwest call it a radical takeover. The university president asks to meet. I tell him only if the press is present. He claims it's his duty to protect us from ourselves. I say I've been taking care of myself and family for years. He says Most students are younger and need supervision. I say When we lived down the street from you, faculty and administration folks stumbled out of your parties after midnight so drunk and loud they woke us up, so age has nothing to do with it. He gets all flustered as flashbulbs pop.

39

I talk the university into letting me take more courses for more credits than was ever allowed before. Then into letting me be the first student they let work on a BA and MFA at the same time. But first I have to be accepted into the graduate Poetry Workshop. I'm told Marvin Bell argues against it saying, like Tate, my poetry is too raw. The deciding vote is George Starbuck's who says he thinks the workshop students, most from elite schools, will benefit from being in classes with a working-class veteran whose poems are too raw. A little mag lit critic classifies me with some other little mag poets, like Doug Blazek and Charles Bukowski, as *The Raw Meat School of Poetry*.

40

Ginsberg comes to Iowa for *GENTLE THURS-DAY*, an attempt to create a hippie holiday. Grad poet Ken McCullough, who lives in a cabin in the woods, throws a party for him, with a pig roasting on a spit over a burning pit. It's there I watch two white jocks slap hands in greeting as only hip spades and jazz musicians did just a few years ago, when only slightly longer hair was a demarcation line between hip and square. Now even longer locks, like McCullough's, are becoming common. Like me, he had a life before Iowa, playing minor league base-ball, or so I hear. Ginsberg doesn't seem to re-member me from my Greenwich Village days.

41

Among friends from Africa, Asia, and South America in the International Workshop, I'm closest to Cambodian poet U Sam Oeur. On first hearing me read my poetry he says Too much shit. I think he means extraneous ideas or images. But he means the actual word: *Shit.* He says There's enough shit in the world. He grew up in rural Cambodia riding on the backs of water buffalos in rice paddies, listening to his father's stories about encountering ghosts on his way home drunk. Sam reminds me of my Irish peasant immigrant grandparents. Though he's experienced much more of the world than they ever did. Including Iowa City.

42

I love U Sam's pure spirit, his dedication to his principles and people, and his love of poetry. He feels, as I do, that poetry saved his life. In a memoir he'll write: *I formed a particular bond with Mike Lally...he could run circles around anyone when talking politics...I recall in a discussion about Ho Chi Minh, Michael made Uncle Ho seem like Mother Theresa...on the surface we were exact opposites, but on the inside we were brothers.* Years later back in Cambodia when Pol Pot takes over, Sam will bury poems near his home, chop his hair, tear his clothes, and smear shit on them, to be taken for a crazy man not an intellectual. It'll work: he'll survive.

43

I hold Lee's hand for hours as she labors quietly, only a string of curses under her breath at the recurring pain. We can hear a woman singing arias that get louder and louder til her singing becomes screaming. It scares Lee but also makes her laugh between contractions. Eventually they make me wait in the room where fathers pace, as in all the cartoons and movies, till Caitlin is shown to me behind glass, in an incubator cause she's so small. I always found newborns with their pinched little faces alike and wondered how people could line up and stare at the little monkeys for hours. Now I know.

44

After being in the hospital all day with Lee and Cait, I go to Kenney's at night. The juke box keeps playing Procul Harem's *WHITER SHADE OF PALE* over and over. Everyone seems to know it's my latest favorite song. The whole bar toasts me for the baby. But I don't drink, so poet Eric T invites a few of us to his pad to get high. A sweet, soft-spoken guy, he puts on some old 45s as we toke up. When poet Steve Shrader's art-student girlfriend, Sylvia Schuster, shows up, she tries to get me to dance. She grew up in Philly where her sister and she boogied on the original AMERICAN BANDSTAND and knows the words to all the old songs.

45

Sylvia is voluptuous with long flowing dark hair but dresses in what looks like a bum's old pants and a couple of mangy sweaters. She constantly puts her hair up, and takes it down, wraps it to one side, and otherwise reconfigures it during any encounter. An instant friend, it's a relief to be not just understood but appreciated in a way only she seems able to do. She tells tales of Irish bad boys she knew, growing up a smart Jewish girl near a Catholic school. When she knocks on our door wanting to see the baby, Lee lets her watch Cait sleep, sure me and this woman, sexy even in layers of old men's clothes and covered with print-making stains, are having an affair. We aren't.

46

When Martin Luther King is shot I feel the sudden shift in the atmosphere, like trying to breathe underwater. It's been three years since Malcom X's assassination and my new radical friends and reading have opened my eyes to the realities of class in the USA. Malcolm verbally attacked white folks with impunity, but the minute he decided it was not about race but about the poor and the wealthy, BAM! King spent years fighting racism and despite attempts on his life and tons of threats seemed invulnerable, but as soon as he organized a poor people's campaign talking about the haves and have-nots, BAM! I wonder if the Marxists have it right.

47

In Harry Duncan's book-arts class I design, print, and bind *A BESTIARY FOR CAITLIN*, a selection of poems by me and others to her. Spanish Harry comes out to be godfather at her Baptism. At the party after, in our pad, Michael Dennis Brown, U Sam Ouer, Ray, Tim Steffa, Canadian poet Wayne Clifford and his wife Julie, the Suttons, and Finnish-born poet Anselm Hollo, who arrived with flowers for Cait he confesses he stole from in front of a bank, improvise till dawn on kazoos, guitars, and pots and pans. Next day Harry and I catch up, me trying to convince him Marxism makes sense. He isn't buying.

48

Despite exterminator visits, one morning I find cockroaches crawling over Caitlin in her crib even her face. We move to married student housing, Quonset huts from World War Two shaped like semi-circles with rippled outlines of corrugated metal that reverberate loudly when it rains, and become a kind of torture when it hails, once as big as snowballs. Every Quonset hut houses a family on each end with a thin wall between. On the other end of ours is workshop poet David Drum and wife, Janice. With no children, but a TV, they often babysit for us. From Southern California, even in Iowa winters he wears the baggies and huaraches The Beach Boys sing about.

49

I start working for Kim Merker's Stone Wall and Windhover Presses, hand printing and binding books at night, at times deep into the early morning hours, and also take a job at THE PAPER PLACE. So I'm able to quit the home repair jobs and unloading trucks. I also write movie and music reviews for *THE DAILY IOWAN* and a political column called *UNDER THE TEA*, riffing off *THE DES MOINES REGISTER* column called *OVER A COFFEE*, my editors missing, or maybe not, the nod to being under the influence of weed. I write for *THE IOWA DEFENDER* too, and all kinds of underground and alternative rags.

50

Some radicals and less political hippies start a Free University where I teach radical tomes I've been studying on my own, even Stalin's, probably written by others. I don't dig him but figure people should know what all the Commies we were taught to demonize have to say. The Progressive Labor faction of SDS, the furthest left group on campus, smart kids whose arguments often convince, throw a party and invite me to it. Showing up in my best party clothes I find them in the work shirts and jeans they think workers wear to party. When one confides they're celebrating the assassination of RFK, I split, dismayed.

51

Civil Rights activists continue to be beaten, jailed, and killed, even teenagers, like Bobby Hutton in Oakland, California, where The Black Panthers get national attention when Huey Newton leads them into the streets with shotguns to monitor police activities, often ending in shootouts. They invade the state capital in Sacramento carrying their guns to confront state legislators with the legality of their activities, since the state constitution allows for unconcealed long arms in public. I write an article about them and am asked to speak about them on panels, until an Iowa chapter forms and they speak for themselves.

52

Because I've gained notice as an anti-war activist, men younger than me ask me to recommend them for conscientious objector status. I write and speak out about how student deferments mean working-class or poor kids get drafted to fight in their place, so only reluctantly do I write the recommendations, encouraged by my mentor Fred Stover, from the FDR administration, now the gray-haired leader of a radical farmers group whose newspaper I write for and meetings I speak at. His first vote was for socialist Eugene Debs when Debs ran for president from jail in 1920.

53

In June 1968 I get a BA in English and Asian Studies, while still working on an MFA in poetry. On graduation day, with a crew of manual laborers in the back of a pickup riding to a moving job for extra money, we pass a long line of students in caps and gowns. I feel sad for a minute for not being with them, then think how cooked they look in those outfits and how I hate dressing up now that I'm not the hip jazzman anymore. Lots of friends graduate and move on. Slater to San Francisco, Ray to teach college in Ohio. And Eric T, who leaves behind for us his '54 Chevy on its last legs, or wheels.

54

I buy brushes and paints and when friends drop by ask them to make art on the blue and white Chevy. On the right front fender Shrader paints a topless female scuba diver amid exotic colorful fish. Others paint lines from poems, quotes from philosophers and revolutionaries, or abstract patterns. A traveling art exhibition that I drive, full of friends, to a party in a cabin Darrell Gray rents with other poets. When we arrive, *SUMMERTIME* is blasting into the hot night air, sung by an old, black, female blues singer I can't identify. Turns out it's a young white hippie girl, Janis Joplin, on the new album: *CHEAP THRILLS*.

55

Redhead writer George Kimball has a needle he got from the hospital with adrenalin they shoot into patients whose hearts have stopped. He jabs it into his chest and slams to the floor, shaking like a cartoon character being electrocuted. A few of us do what we do when someone OD's, we pull the needle out, lift him under the arms and walk him around outside til the shaking stops and he seems back to being high but not totally incapacitated. Kimball is notorious for his glass eye, which he loves to slip out of its socket and into your drink when you aren't looking, so when you go to take a sip, his fake eye looks up at you from the bottom of the glass.

56

When we get out of the party at dawn, the Chevy won't start. We try everything, but no go. Somehow I get home and then am so busy with part-time jobs, classes, politics, writing poetry and fiction and reviews, and political columns for a few papers, teaching and more, it's a week before I get a ride out to retrieve the Chevy. When we arrive, my work-of-art vehicle is gone. I walk to where the farmer sits on his tractor and ask about my car. He says I pushed it into a ditch and plowed it under for fill. My anger doesn't bother him at all. The car was left on his property, so he did what he saw fit to a unique work of art he only saw as a hunk of junk or offensive affront.

57

Kimball and some stoned friends stop by our Quonset hut on their way to pick up poet Anselm Hollo at the Cedar Rapids Airport. People are always coming and going to the airport. I have a giant roll of newsprint about three feet high I found in the street one day, so I cut off ten feet of it and give colored markers to everyone to make a banner we can hold up at the airport as Anselm deplanes. Helplessly paralyzed with stonedness, no one comes up with anything. When the flight lands we unfurl our blank banner for Anselm to see when he comes down the steps from the plane. But he isn't among the departing passengers. Which seems profound to us: a banner saying nothing for nobody.

58

I find a used, Army-green, telephone-company truck for sale, racks on top, metal shelves and drawers inside, and go to a grad workshop poet I know comes from money, Geoff Hewitt, to borrow the three hundred. He writes out a check on the spot. I feel guilty for all my petty envy of his financial security. He's so generous and human about it I don't even feel I'm imposing. I can park it anywhere and get no tickets, cops assuming the driver is repairing a phone line nearby. I take out the shelves and racks and put an old mattress in back and repay the loan in a few months.

59

When Ken W and I pick Tom Hayden up from the airport to take him to his hotel room, he invites us in to talk, but has to make a long distance call and gets belligerently impatient with the operator. Thinking of someone talking to my wife that way I confront him and we argue. At one point he says something like The People are too backward to lead a revolution or govern themselves, they need leaders, like us. Attempting to include us in, in what seems to Ken and me an obviously manipulative maneuver to get us to see things his way. We don't. Later, in the middle of his speech to a packed auditorium on campus there's a loud explosion and smoke, panicking the audience.

60

Everyone figures it's a bomb, but the smoke coming from the vents has the familiar odor of tear gas to me. As Hayden is hustled out, I get Lee and Cait to the exit, then signal Ken to follow my lead as I jump on a chair to shout IT'S JUST TEAR GAS, MOVE SLOWLY TO THE EXITS. And they do. When we take Cait to the university hospital, the nurse is sweet, til we tell her we were at a speech where tear gas went off. She goes from friendly to cold, blaming us for taking a baby to a peacenik rally. Lee tells her she's confused if she believes an innocent baby deserves to be tear gassed for being near someone speaking against the war.

61

The difference between '67 and '68 is
like a kiss and a shootout to a lot of us,
though some of us are aware it's been
no kiss for many folks ever. The Summer
of Love and The Summer of Revolution.
But that doesn't keep us from grooving.
Lee makes brownies, cookies, even tea,
with pot in them, for us and visitors
though not on the summer day my sister
Irene and husband visit with their first
born, Cait's baby cousin. When a car
hits and kills a wild rabbit in front of our
Quonset hut, with only the head damaged
Lee skins it, cooks it, and eats it. I don't.

62

The Peace and Freedom Party comes to Iowa
when some of us start a state branch. I write
most of the platform and pamphlets and flyers.
When we discuss challenging the sheriff of
Johnson County with our own nominee, I'm
chosen but turn it down, three times, instead
suggesting we put the entire party on the ballot
for sheriff. When they vote a fourth time for
me, I finally agree. At the convention in Ann
Arbor I meet Panther Bobby Seale—the night-
club MC I identify with more than I do with
Huey Newton or Eldridge Cleaver—and argue
tactics with Tom Hayden, who's calling for a
protest at the Democratic Convention in Chicago.

63

When Eldridge Cleaver wins the Peace and Freedom Party nomination for president, I move to have Peggy Terry as his running mate. Cleaver wants Jerry Rubin. Peggy, a middle-aged, anti-war, anti-poverty activist from Chicago's hillbilly ghetto, grew up in Kentucky and lived in Alabama, so poor and back country she married at fourteen a fellow teen who died in the mine he worked in. She likes to point out their wedding was presided over by then Justice of the Peace George Wallace before he became the segregationist governor running for president. After a lot of arguing about it, Cleaver calls for a recess.

64

In a small room Cleaver meets with a handful of Panther, SDS, and Peace and Freedom leaders. A young Panther who carries around newly cleaned and pressed shirts helps Cleaver change into one as he continues to insist Jerry Rubin be his running mate. I say Rubin is a joke to working people I know, while Peggy Terry is one of them and can appeal to older whites who are afraid of Cleaver, but who do most of the voting. Cleaver orders some young Panthers to throw me out of the meeting. I say Fuck that man, this isn't a dictatorship. But they pick me up and carry me out. Later the party compromises, letting each state choose its own vice-presidential candidate.

65

The Iowa Peace and Freedom party runs Peggy Terry for vice president. Other states run Jerry Rubin, who with Abbie Hoffman and the Yippie Party run a pig for president, a joke my working-class clan and friends don't get. The media focuses on the pig, ignoring Cleaver and Terry. Peggy comes to Iowa for some of our rallies when she can. At one she misses, I meet Mike J who comes down from Chicago in her place. We spend all night talking activism. His father is a Broadway producer, but Mike fell in love with Chicago, and its working class and poor, while he was on a football scholarship to Lake Forrest and dedicated his life to helping them.

66

With Roy and Karen gone, Dave and Ilya become my political advisors. Red Diaper Babies raised by parents who were in The Communist Party, or sympathizers, going to summer camps where they sang leftist anthems and learned how capitalists exploit workers, they have a way of defusing my most extreme political enthusiasms with the reality of their personal history of the left and its foibles. Meanwhile any sympathy I retain for communism disappears when Soviet troops and tanks invade Czechoslovakia. Another East Coast Jewish lefty, Mark, drops by at all hours to talk tactics. If we are sleeping, he sits smoking in our second-hand rocking chair, our only place to sit, til we wake up.

67

As a college-student radical running for sheriff I get noticed by local and regional papers, even *THE WALL STREET JOURNAL*. I'm asked to speak to groups from The Chamber of Commerce to The Quakers, and on radio and TV all over the Midwest, one week giving five speeches. Kimball wants to get me more national publicity, but I'm not into making it about me this time. Speaking to a crowd at the old capitol building, Caitlin asleep peacefully against my chest, her head resting on my shoulder as I address them, a photographer takes a photo that appears in several papers the next day of Cait's sweet little face, eyes closed, against my neck. Dave warns me I'm endangering my family.

68

SDS tests a new university injunction against using a live microphone at outdoor rallies, Ken and Jerry S the testers. The next day's paper has a photo of me at the microphone while The Associate Dean attempts to hand me a copy of the injunction I refuse. He had told the crowd anyone speaking on the mic will be arrested or expelled. Flashing on *SPARTACUS*, I get up to the mic and, as *THE DAILY IOWAN* reports, remind people of that movie, telling them Ken and Jerry won't be arrested or expelled if we all step up to the mic and one at a time say our names into it, til there are too many of us to kick out. It works, as hundreds do just that.

69

An article in a Cedar Rapids paper calls me A*n*
apostle of the New Left… preach[ing] *its gospel.*
Then misquotes me, using phrases I'd never say
like *The rise of the working class.* But others
sound close, as when the reporter writes: *Lally,*
husband, father, poet, Air Force veteran and
student says, I want a world where love is
more possible and where all…have…respect
for each other. I want things to…change…so
when my daughter grows up she won't have
to face the issues we face now. But it, too, has
a photo of me. Dave warns me again that I'm
making myself and my family a target for right-
wingers. He knows what he's talking about.

70

In a grange hall full of farmers, way out in rural
Johnson County in what's called WALLACE
COUNTRY, cause most there support George
Wallace for president, I walk onto the stage
and stand there, letting them take a good long
look at my shoulder length hair, then say: I can
guess what a lot of you are thinking. Why doesn't
this guy get a haircut? Pause. I'll tell you why.
I spent four years in the military getting my hair
cut by the numbers, which any vet knows is doing
it the way the brass want it, and an hour before
I was about to be discharged, an officer made me
get a haircut. I vowed then I'd never get another
one til I felt like it. And I haven't felt like it yet.

71

The sheriff I'm running against spoke before I did, passing out photos of long-haired students at a protest, claiming they were Communist agitators. I tell the farmer audience: If the family of cops I come from, or my seventh-grade-drop-out father, or even me before I became a college student on the G. I. Bill, saw these photos, we'd think those students look like Commie radicals too, but after I became a student I found out they're just good kids whose government is urging them to support a war, or drafting them into it, fought on what they're learning are false assumptions and outright lies, and when they use their right to protest against that, they're attacked and arrested.

72

After speaking to the farmers, many come up to shake my hand and tell me how much they got out of what I had to say. One farm couple asks me to their home for dinner. Later I'll get letters from others inviting me to visit their farms and towns. A lot of the men, all veterans, admit agreeing with some of my perspective. But one farmer is the embodiment of what the left has to face. He's a WWII vet whose platoon had captured some Germans during a battle. He says They was pretty much like us 'cept for babblin' their own gibberish, but they were plain white men like you and me, now these Vietnamese, they're more like monkeys than men ain't they?

73

Mike J slicks his blonde hair back greaser style, as they call it in Chicago, and wears a three-quarter length black leather coat, same as my own. Known as an SDS leader nationally, after *LIFE* did a story on him, he has an idea for organizing Chicago's white gang kids into a radical street organization and wants me to join him. We begin spending more time in Chicago and discover he not only runs with the Black Panthers, and white street gangs, and sons of hillbilly immigrants from the South, but also moves with ease among the liberal elite of the city, raising money and backers for the cause. I'm at home among the street kids not the rich.

74

Mike takes Lee and me to Chicago blues clubs to hear Junior Walker and other favorites of hers she's never heard live. When he takes us to a wealthy fundraising friend's cocktail party, I get high and say to the white hostess Sweet joint ya got here sister. And: Ain't life a bitch? My stoned gravelly Miles Davis voice edging toward verbal aggression from feeling out of place, and angry at feeling that way. When a wealthy liberal tells us he'll pay for plastic surgery for Lee, she's insulted by it, as she always is. Mike tries to get her to see the rich cat is only trying to help her, but she never wants to go back to Chicago and Mike's friends. And doesn't. I start going alone.

75

After one Chicago fund raising party, riding
to Mike's pad on his motorcycle, me on back,
both in our leathers, he pulls over and gets
off the cycle to stand before a foundry gate
that blocks entry but lets the sweet night air
through. It's a sight I've never seen, but
Mike is used to, yet still mesmerized by.
Hot molten steel pouring from giant vats like
lava from an active volcano, glowing bright
red and orange, lighting up the night, hot
enough to make my face feel sunburned
standing there in our tough guy outfits, the
hog behind us, watching these true working-
class stiffs pour hot steel on the night shift.

76

When Peggy Terry stays with us on a trip to
Iowa City, Lee tells her how we argue over
whether we will contribute our copper kettle
if the metal is needed to keep people poorer
than us warm in winter. Lee says she'd do it for
friends but not strangers who didn't help us get
it in the first place. Peggy tells us how one of
her sisters felt ashamed to let Peggy know she
got a new coat, for fear Peggy would criticize
her for being booshie. Peggy cries talking about
it, then takes Lee in her arms to say Oh honey
it's okay to want nice things, this isn't about
making everybody poor, this is about getting
poor people the same nice things others have.

77

Ted Berrigan, recently profiled in *NEWSWEEK* as the Pied Piper to the hippies of Manhattan's East Village, comes to teach in the Poetry Workshop. Dena Polansky and Robert Harris invite us for dinner to meet him and his wife Sandy. Ted claims he heard of me as the teenage white kid with the black girlfriend when he first arrived in New York. I express anger at Kerouac's pro-war stance, calling hippies commies in an interview Ted did with him in the new *PARIS REVIEW*. Ted says any writer who can describe eating a hamburger as well as Kerouac, can say whatever he wants to.

78

From behind the high counter at THE PAPER PLACE, I'm knocking *BEAN SPASMS*, Ted Berrigan's book with Ron Padgett, to some students when I realize Ted has walked in and is overhearing me. I'm saying stoned word play, paid for by rich patrons while the world burns, is a self-indulgent cop-out. He asks what's wrong with having a little fun, giving people some relief from the depressing news. We argue, but recognizing we're fellow Irish-American East Coast working-class military veterans who did college on the G.I. Bill become close. He wants to know why a poet like me is in Iowa and not back in New York City.

79

Kurt Vonnegut always treats me as an equal. Not Robert Coover, who teaches in the grad Fiction Workshop where he tells me I'm too social and political to ever be a successful novelist. But at a huge campus event against the war, he reads a story he dedicates to me for running for sheriff and standing up to the powers that be to protest the war. More and more professors and students are against the war. At the biggest anti-war march in Iowa City yet, Ken and I start singing that song from the movie *MARAT/SADE: Marat we're poor and the poor stay poor.* And the entire march starts singing along with us.

80

The party after a Diane Wakoski reading is at Ted Berrigan's house where I talk stoned into her ear for more than a half hour, as she keeps nodding her bird head and politely smiling as though my stoned rap about Newark versus New York Poets is really pleasing her, but I'm thinking all the time she's just watching Bill Knott sit stoned in Ted's barber chair with stereo earphones over his crewcut head, eyes closed. Knott gives me his copy of Nazim Hikmet's selected poems and asks why I'm in Iowa. I tell him cause I want a degree in poetry to prove to critics that I know what I'm doing in my own poetry. He says he doubts it'll work.

81

When I discover my mail is being opened, I confront the postmaster of Iowa City, who claims it isn't, but it begins arriving on time and without so obviously having been tampered with. Then I start getting rightwing threats in the mail. One has a drawing of a rifle site and the warning that I'll never know when I answer the door or turn the key in my van or get gas for it, whether that'll be when the bomb goes off or the sniper's bullet pierces my brain. Dave doesn't say I told you so, but advises me to step back, let others take the lead at rallies and protests. I do, after the election, where I come in second in the vote for sheriff.

82

When John Lennon gets divorced, Lee gets angry at me, convinced I'm gonna do the same, cause the publicity I get has been attracting women she feels I'll leave her for. We use Christmas break to visit the Wilsons in Berkeley, Shrader and Salner along to help with driving. We have the mattress in the back of the telephone van to sleep on, in shifts, while Cait's playpen doubles as a crib. In Nebraska we hit a blizzard. Traffic slows to a few miles an hour, then stops. National Guard troops lead us to a truck stop, where we find a booth and let some Mexicans squeeze in to wait with us in that friendly shared-disaster way. We nap sitting up all night. Cait sleeps on the table.

83

At dawn, National Guard troops tell us we can leave soon. We take turns going to the restrooms to clean up, Shrader and I washing when two truck drivers enter the men's room. One sarcastically comments to the other he thinks he's in the ladies' room. Shrader's hair is longer than mine, but he has a goatee I point out to the guy angrily. Shrader grabs my arm and pulls me out saying Ignore them Michael, they're just intimidated by anything they don't understand. And reminds me to think of Lee and Caitlin. Back on the highway we see big wood-slatted trucks with their back doors open, and out in the snowdrifts: cattle, hair iced, breath creating clouds of steam, still alive.

84

Trying to get over Donner Pass we end up in another blizzard. Troopers turn us back to Reno where we get a cheap funky motel room for Lee and me and the baby, Shrader and Salner in another, the telephone van too cold to sleep in it. We find the situation a little bit ironic, a little bit poignant, having trouble finding better accommodations on Christmas Eve with Lee and our baby. In the morning we try again, with the required tire chains this time. Salner and Shrader sit over the back wheels to add their weight. We make it over the pass, then drop the two of them in Frisco and go on to the Wilsons in Berkeley.

85

In Frisco we spend time with Ralph Dickey and see Lewis MacAdams, working as a barker for the North Beach strip joint that features Carol Doda, my AWOL neighborhood now a glutted tourist trap, and meet Lewis's wife, the legendary beauty Phoebe, and discuss tactics and upcoming protests with Oakland SDS activists. Later we drive to Bolinas to look for blonde Sue, old friend from South Orange who Charlie almost left his wife for. After her parents sent her to Italy to forget him, she came home with an Italian husband and they moved to the hippie haven. But she isn't anywhere to be found this day.

86

I have to get back to classes and jobs, so to avoid more snow we take the Southern route through the desert and Needles, fellow workshop poet Alice Notley's hometown. Seeing it, makes her more understandable, the usually quiet beauty with the big doe eyes. Continuing through the desert in the dark, lying on the mattress with Lee asleep, I notice red lights reflected on the ceiling and tell Shrader, who's driving, to pull over. When he does, the back and side doors are flung open by men with pistols drawn, some in uniform, some not. One yells GET OUT WITH YOUR HANDS UP! NOW! And we do our best to comply.

87

Standing in the cold dessert night air, I start to slide my hands into my pockets. One of the pistol pointing men screams KEEP YOUR HANDS UP! I tell the obvious leader of the group, while he checks our I.D.s, that I come from a family of cops. He just scowls, and returning our I.D.s tells us to Get outta here. I say You made us stand out here with guns in our faces, we got a right to know what's goin' on. He says We're looking for a gang of desert hippies who murdered some people. When The Manson Family atrocities are revealed a few months later, I figure it must have been them the posse was looking for.

88

Chris Parker is a film-student star, who won a prestigious national award for a short movie. His square-jawed handsomeness reminds me of Superman in the comics when I was a boy. He's the first person I ever hear use the term demagogue, and he's referring to me. I like him anyway. He asks me to play what he thinks is myself in *WHITEY!* the first feature funded by The American Film Institute. I tell him to replace the poster of Martin Luther King on the wall of what's supposed to be the radicals' meeting place with one of Malcolm X. He just adds the Malcolm X instead. He shoots some scenes at our Quonset hut with Lee and Caitlin.

89

At a packed SDS meeting I notice a bespectacled cocoa-colored man exit with a blonde coed and follow them into the hall. It's Gene, my soulmate from the service I haven't seen in six years. He says he was just telling the blonde about us. She doesn't believe our running into each other is just a coincidence. Chris Parker puts Gene in his movie *WHITEY!* too, which won't be shown for a year after it's finished cause David Sundance, a mixed-race friend in the flick, suffers a breakdown and is institutionalized before Parker gets his release signed. Gene stays around for a while before returning to his VISTA gig. Sundance'll run for sheriff too, after he gets out and I've left.

90

Suzanne Burgess has taken over our old pad at Moffet's, and when I stop by to see her she's listening to opera, walking around the crib on mattresses she's laid down in the living room as furniture. She, Ted Berrigan, and me get buzzed and go see *CAMELOT*, the movie, but are too high to stay. Ted leaves first. Then Suzanne. Me last, after feeling for the first time like I'm watching people in front of a camera and under lights, the entire artifice of movie making as apparent as the reality that I'm seeing light and colors projected onto a screen. Anselm is Ted's best friend, but Ted confides in me too that he's leaving Sandy.

91

Gary Snyder comes to Iowa City for the publication of *REGARDING WAVE* for which I set the type by hand, crease the pages with a decades-worn piece of bone, and help sew the folios. I escort him around town looking for a shoe repair shop where he borrows a tool to fix his leather bag as he sits cross legged on the floor of the store. Later at the party, he talks to Ted B and ignores me. My boss Kim pointing to me, drunkenly tells Snyder You know who this is? The man who slaved for weeks setting type for your book. You know how hard it is to match cold type with your typewriter games? You should be on your knees to him. I have to drive Kim home in his little sports car after he passes out.

92

Lee, pregnant again, is in the hospital to have a cyst removed while I spend hours in the print shop cutting pages of *REGARDING WAVE* for Snyder to sign, and he insists the smartest thing I can do for my poetry and family is to move to land he bought in the Sierra Nevadas and help him finish building a house for his family and then build one for mine. He's treating me like an equal now but can't fathom why I want to live in New York City. I tell him I miss the dazzling greens and reds of traffic lights against the strips of deepening dusk blue sky over the cross streets there. He doesn't get it, but when we're done, does his calligraphy magic to write out one of his poems to give Lee.

93

Poets are always visiting Ted, which is how I first meet Peter Schjeldahl and Lewis Mac-Adams. Ted thinks Lewis's and my poetry have things in common, Lewis doesn't. Peter asks why I'm not in New York. At his reading he includes his *PARIS SONNETS* inspiring me to distill the pages of prose on my early life into twenty fourteen-liners I call *THE SOUTH ORANGE SONNETS*, supporting my belief that my own life is just as important as any world traveler's. Ted has me send poems to Anne Waldman for her magazine. She rejects them, so I replace her name for my poems and send the transformed rejections back to her.

94

As Ted's first year of teaching at the workshop comes to an end, he's not asked back. Rumor has it Marvin Bell is envious of Ted's popularity. Bell asks Ted to do a farewell reading with him, and Ted offers to go first. I design and edit a page of *THE DAILY IOWAN* devoted to Ted and his work. A huge crowd shows up. Ted's a great reader, humorous and inclusive. The crowd loves it. But after a while it's clear he's reading maybe everything he's ever written. Bell sits behind him, his smile growing tighter as the time passes and people dribble out, til almost no one's left and it has turned into a grimace. Ted introduces Bell as if all's normal.

95

For the SDS convention in Chicago I get an old style D.A. haircut to avoid hassles with so-called hardhats who attack hippies and anti-war protestors regularly and the police let them. I don't want distractions or arrests. But at the door of the convention, me and Ken are stopped, suspected of being undercover cops, til Mike J vouches for us. When a black speaker verbally whips SDS for being mostly white college kids, I yell SDS should be proud of their stand against racism and the war. But I'm shouted down. When he talks about pussy-whipped men, and how Pussy Power means women getting horizontal and using their pussies for political ends, women start yelling.

96

Mark Rudd, SDS poster boy, literally, his photo on a poster with blood pouring down his face after the student strike at Columbia University turned into a police riot, grew up in South Orange and went to the high school behind my house. But he wasn't part of my neighborhood, so to me he's a rich kid whose hand feels like a dead fish when we shake. I dig, and am impressed with sexy smart Bernadine Dohrn, who's style and personality are almost theatrical. The convention is meant to heal the factionalism in SDS but ends up creating more, splitting into two main camps, some I know joining up with what's becoming known as The Weathermen.

97

Ken W and I visit Chicago to help Mike J with the white street gangs he's organizing. At one party they throw, some young toughs are challenging each other to see how much they can drink and one challenges me. When I say I got nothin' to prove son, and walk away, a dude my age follows me to a couch where we sit down with his girl between us and all share a joint. He's a dark-haired, thin, hip, street cat who surprises me when a Doors record comes on and he leans over to catch my eye and say: I know I ain't queer but when I seen Jim Morrison live, I wondered for a minute. We both laugh.

98

A brotherhood of dealers set up a giant outdoor rock festival outside Iowa City and hire me and Ken for security. The event is just a front for them to bring in the first loads of Sunshine, a new acid, for distribution around the Midwest. Ken and I stand around in the trailer on the site looking bad while the deal is negotiated, then we're asked to make sure everyone pays to get in. Some hippies try to jump the fence but I turn them back. When they express disappointment in me, I say It's a job and I got a growing family to support. They curse me out. After a while of feeling guilty I let crashers climb the fence.

99

Mike J wants me in Chicago to help with *RISING UP ANGRY*, the paper he's starting for the street kids he's radicalizing. I'll become one of the main contributors, under various names. Berrigan and Schjeldahl encourage us to move back to New York. Others to come to San Francisco to join Movement efforts there. Our artist friend Miguel Conde and his wife, now in Sitges, Spain, want us there. Lee insists I have a job lined up before we leave Iowa City and cries til I agree. The head of the new Associated Writing Programs, I never met, kindly recommends me for a creative writing teaching gig at Trinity College in DC, a Catholic girls school run by nuns who hire me sight unseen.

100

The last book I handset the type for is Ezra Pound's *DRAFTS AND FRAGMENTS OF CANTOS*. I write and design the entire final issue of *MIDDLE EARTH*, get my poems into *TRI-QUARTERLY* and other literary journals to prove I can, publish *POEMS OF THE PEOPLE* a mimeo that gets protest poetry from around the country to underground papers to use, write *FROM THE CAMPGROUNDS* a political column for *CAMPUS UNDERGROUND* later *NEW PRAIRIE PRIMER*, get my poems and articles in underground rags like *THE GREAT SPECKLED BIRD* in Atlanta and *THE HELIX* in Seattle where Roxie and Sandy have moved. Driving to DC the radio says Woodstock is now free. We decide to go but after hours long traffic jams, change our minds.

THE HYATTSVILLE SONNETS

"Our responsibilities did not begin
in dreams, though they began in bed."

—Frank O'Hara

1

We stay in the basement of the head of Trinity's English Department, a white-haired English lady, gracious and generous, while we look for a place and the money to pay for it before classes start and my first paycheck comes. I ask my brother Buddy, a junior high principal in Maryland for a loan. He offers me two weeks substitute teaching instead. He started as a high school music teacher, whose marching bands played New York's Macy's Thanksgiving and Miami's Orange Bowl parades while he earned a Masters degree in night school between nightclub gigs. Kids like him, or at least respect him, though he's a strict disciplinarian and uses outdated expressions, like Bobbysoxers.

2

Trinity is across the road from Catholic U. where Buddy went on the G.I. Bill after World War Two. Back then he was my favorite sibling, a wise-cracking reed man playing in hep Swing bands, breaking the DC color line on city buses with his friend, the piano player Don Shirley, marrying the accordion player in a wartime all-girl band, an Italian-American beauty he traveled post-war Europe with in a show that made them want to settle down. Offered the first clarinet chair with the Cleveland Orchestra, our old man convinced him it wasn't a secure enough job. So he plays gigs behind friends like Pearl Bailey and goes to night school, working toward a PhD.

3

Only one place will rent to us when they see
Lee's pregnant. Over the DC line in Hyattsville.
Garden apartments with no gardens, surrounded
by streets wide as highways but no sidewalks.
Our tiny balcony overlooks an intersection of
multi-lane roads with a constant traffic buzz.
Next door lives a Navy recruiter Nam vet and
his beehive hairdo wife and baby boy. In the air
shaft outside our tiny bathroom you can hear a
woman yell at her teenage daughter several times
a day, and night. Lee befriends a self-reliant
mother-of-many refugee from Appalachia, like
in Lee's favorite book *THE DOLLMAKER*. And
me a young Viet Nam veteran telephone lineman.

4

We sleep on a mattress on the floor, Cait in her
crib, and eat on my brother Buddy's Navy foot-
locker passed on to me as a boy, which I hoped
to always live my life so everything I owned
could fit in. But married with two kids, that
ain't working. Eventually, from the Good Will
store, we get a kitchen table and chairs, and a
couch we drape an American flag over, my
Aunt Mary won't sit on when she visits, but
also doesn't criticize us for. We hang the 1964
TIME cover of Thelonious Monk Lee framed, a
John Hanor painting, and Sylvia Schuster print,
and some posters, but I still feel like one of the
animals I refuse to ever go see caged in zoos.

5

Some of my students are daughters of diplomats and government luminaries, including Senators. Most graduated from Catholic high schools where they learned to follow rules. I give assignments they find so unexpected they come to me in tears pleading for more traditional ones. But it's almost 1970, even the nuns aren't wearing their old habits anymore. One Irish-American student, Martina Darragh, reminds me of family. Head of the Young Republicans, she quickly becomes more adventurous in politics and writing, partly inspired, with me, by Francis Ponge's *SOAP*. In our pad we have an oversized postcard pic of Brando in *THE WILD ONES* a babysitter student thinks is me.

6

Whatever remnant of Beat coffee-house-poetry-reading scene DC had is gone by the time I get there. The only poetry readings are at The Library of Congress and local universities and colleges where the local poets all seem to teach. I'm put up for a poetry award from what will soon become The National Endowment for the Arts, but arriving at the party celebrating it, at Siv Cedering Fox's luxurious home, I'm met by embarrassment and confusion. She explains they thought I was a Negro. The prize goes to a black poet. I'm invited to join a poetry salon in the home of a poetry professor where everyone is white and accomplished but too sedate for me.

7

I begin organizing blocks, as greasers are called
in Maryland and DC, against the war. In Chicago
The Weathermen's DAYS OF RAGE, intended
to spark a police reaction some hope will lead to
a protestor's death spurring masses of people to
rise up in revolution, draws only a few hundred.
No deaths but a lot of arrests, among them *RISING
UP ANGRY* and SDS folks I know. In November
a bunch of *RISING UP ANGRY* dudes, in DC for
the biggest anti-war protest so far, stay with us,
sleeping on the floor. I try to set up an anti-war
poetry reading as part of it. Robert Bly and Ed
Sanders agree to show but Ginsberg cancels, the
only poet the organizers know, so they call it off.

8

Nixon surrounds The White House with buses,
armed troops and cops ringing them. At a march
from Dupont Circle that night, little black boys
run out of the dark to smash storefront windows,
jump in, and run off with their loot. Some white
marchers follow their lead. Not us. The cops,
some on horseback, attack with clubs and tear
gas. We retreat to the park in the circle. As the
cops tighten the noose, I tell the Chicago guys
I'll be back, split to my telephone van, open the
side and back doors to drive through the tear gas
and onto the grass in the circle, where they leap
in while I do some adrenaline-fueled wheelman
maneuvers to get us out, even through the cops.

9

Ray DiPalma is staying with us when our son Miles is born on Thanksgiving 1969 at DC's Children's Hospital. After spending the night at the hospital where Lee's in labor, Ray's at our place with our toddler Cait, so I rush home to get her breakfast. By the time I get back, Miles has arrived. Small and underweight he's put in an incubator at first. A woman doctor says he might have water on the brain cause his head is big compared to his tiny body but another doc, a man, says she's an alarmist and our son is just fine. Ray is always our neatest houseguest, leaving no trace of his ever having been here after he's gone away.

10

In December, Fred Hampton, the young charismatic, coalition-building-with-poor-and-working-class-whites, Chicago Black Panther leader I've met and admire, is brutally slaughtered with Panther Mark Clark when police raid Hampton's crib, after firing hundreds of bullets into it, and into him, asleep in his bed. It's the latest demonstration of the cops' and FBI's and other law enforcement agencies' display of arrogant attacks on black leaders. I've objected to Panthers calling police pigs, thinking of cops in my clan who are decent, but this time it seems insulting to actual pigs.

11

The 1970s begin with Nixon's redesign
of the uniforms of the White House guards.
A cross between the marching-band outfits
in *THE MUSIC MAN*, only white not red,
and palace-guard uniforms in an old Jean-
nette MacDonald/Nelson Eddy movie mu-
sical. I write a story incorporating the uni-
forms and a protestor's recent successful
attempt to climb The White House fence
and the percolating push for gay rights,
among some in The Movement, but mostly
the trouble Lee gives me if I don't make
love to her every night without fail, and
call it *I LOST IT AT THE WHITE HOUSE.*

12

At Mike J's Chicago wedding, a mix of money,
THE CHICAGO SEVEN, SDSers, and gangs, I
officiate, with two *RISING UP ANGRY* dudes
in berets and leathers holding shotguns, a la The
Panthers, beside me, the first notes of *GIMME
SHELTER* blasting as I finish. Peggy Terry's
son Youngblood took me for a hillbilly when he
read my review of *THE WILD BUNCH* where I
point out the more redneck the accent the more
evil a character in it is. Learning I need bread
for my flight back to DC, he challenges The
Young Lords and others: Show you ain't fulla
shit, lay down some dust for Lally. Throwing
down a twenty, glaring at anyone holding back.

13

Wilson is in Charlottesville at JAG school for three months. We drive down from DC for a visit and catch The Band in concert with all the Southern frat boys singing *THE NIGHT THEY DROVE OLD DIXIE DOWN* like an anthem. He points out how much the bass player looks like me, or vice versa. Coming back, my old telephone van conks out. It's cold and we're on an upgrade, but I get out and Lee, with baby Miles in her lap, Caitlin in the playpen in back, steers while I push it over the incline, run to the driver's seat and pop the clutch to jump start it. We make it back to DC. Wilson tells me I should get a Toyota wagon. I've never even heard of Toyota.

14

The SDS Weathermen get more and more intense. Then a townhouse on Washington Square blows up with three of them in it messing with bomb making. Not long after that a giant paperback comes out called *THE MOVEMENT TOWARD A NEW AMERICA* with articles, poems, photos, cartoons, and more from the underground and alternative press, including some of my words throughout it, none attributed to me. Like an article from *RISING UP ANGRY* called *PIGS… THE NATURE OF THE BEAST* where I argue that even if we come from police families, the cops no longer work for all of us but only to protect the interests of the powerful and wealthy.

15

In the city to see Cal and Cissie, we stay at The Chelsea Hotel. Suzanne Burgess there with her new older husband Arnold Weinstein who I learn wrote the off-Broadway hit *RED EYE OF LOVE* and remember the poster for it in OBIES. He invites us to see his adaptation of Brecht and Weill's *MAHAGONY*. We ask Alice Notley, living in the city now, to babysit our kids so we can go, but she says she doesn't babysit, then excitedly tells us of famous poets she's been meeting through Ted Berrigan. Suzanne watches the kids so we can go, but I get too stoned before the show and grow paranoid as the musical unfolds.

16

When four students at Kent State in Ohio are killed by National Guardsmen, we see it on our Navy recruiter neighbors' TV, who tells me if we end up on opposite sides of the barricades, he'll shoot only at my legs. Later from our balcony we watch helicopters hover over the not far U of Maryland campus where students are protesting as tear gas drifts toward us. Days later, with ten thousand others I join rallies at The Capitol and White House while students protesting at Jackson State, a black Mississippi college, are shot by cops, killing two and wounding a dozen. The next rally I'm part of is at The Lincoln Memorial where Black Panthers call for a convention to rewrite The Constitution.

17

In our supermarket, Lee runs into a high school friend from Buffalo who invites her to a women's consciousness-raising meeting at the home of a lady with a WASPy married name. In Iowa Lee had been urged by students to take a leading role in the burgeoning Women's Movement but declined. She reluctantly goes to this meeting and comes back to tell me the woman whose home it was at told of falling in love in college with a young poet who fell for a black woman, so she married a WASPy named man and had children but is unhappy and blames it all on the poet. Her name is Angela. Lee figured out the poet is me and decides Angela's anger at me is justified.

18

Sue B is a go-go dancer who organized other go-go dancers into a union fighting for better wages and freedom from their male managers, who are more like pimps. I read about her in *THE WASHINGTON POST* and invite her to speak to my classes at Trinity for them to see someone as young as them facing challenges they never imagined. An editor at Scribner's sees a story of mine in a little mag and asks for a novel I tell him I've written but haven't, so I write one in two weeks, about a Vietnam vet working at a mental institution like Overbrook where he almost goes insane himself and ends up re-enlisting for Nam. They turn it down.

19

Ray publishes the poetry mag, *DOONES*, and decides to put out *WHAT WITHERS*, a slim, side stapled, Xeroxed book of my poems. Another friend publishes a tiny book of my poetry inspired by my kids' attempts at language, a drawing by Caitlin on the cover. In Iowa City, an artfully handmade version of a poem I wrote about Charlotte comes out in a very limited edition. My first books, what some call chapbooks. Not many notice. But Todd Gitlin asks me to send him poems for an anthology called *CAMPFIRES OF THE RESISTANCE: Poetry From The Movement.*

20

In September, The Black Panthers hold a mass meeting to discuss the Revolutionary Peoples Constitutional Convention they plan for DC in November. It draws thousands of people to the preliminary session in Philly at the Temple U gym, where I get to shake Muhammed Ali's hand again as he mingles with us delegates. Later, I make sure Ken W, and those with us, avoid arrest when the Philly cops come down on the radical throng invading their city. Few of us realize this will be the peak of The Black Panthers' influence as the FBI continues its relentless collaboration with police across the country to decimate the Panther leadership.

21

I talk the Trinity nuns into hosting the women who come to DC for The Black Panthers Revolutionary Peoples Convention to Rewrite The Constitution. The nuns and students shocked by fatigue wearing lesbians, radical feminists, and Black Panther women sleeping in dorm rooms and on floors throughout the school. Howard University demands the Panthers deposit ten thousand dollars to use facilities they've been promised, money they can't come up with that fast. After pressure from the FBI, other schools turn them down too. Except for one music concert in the renamed Malcolm X Park that draws thousands, the convention is a bust.

22

The war expanding into Laos and Cambodia, the bombing in Madison taking an innocent life, and the deaths of Jimi Hendrix and Janis Joplin within weeks of each other, depress me. But I continue to declare that poetry has saved my life. Etheridge Knight, in DC for a reading, stays with us. Sent to prison for a heroin habit, while there he won acclaim as a poet, and when he got out became the darling of some prominent literary figures. Tall, dark-toned, and bespectacled, with chin hair he picks at when nodding, an original thinker from rural Mississippi he now lives in Indiana, where he, Anselm Hollo, Ray DiPalma, Robert Slater, and I do a memorable poetry reading over two nights at Wabash College.

23

After Ralph Dickey moves to Syracuse he tries to get me a job where he works, a government-funded educational center for vets and out-of-work blue collar folks. But they don't want a white male. The country is just as white-male dominated as ever, but on the left a strong resistance to the white patriarchy is growing. When I apply to be the poetry editor at *MOTIVE*, a slick Christian mag fast becoming more politically left, they say they have to turn me down cause I'm a white male. When I tell Etheridge Knight, he says he always thinks of me as a black poet. I recommend him for the job and he gets it.

24

Visiting Ted and Alice in The City, Ted gives us a hardcover copy of his new book *IN THE EARLY MORNING RAIN*. He's been given last minute tickets to a Knicks game, so I drive them to The Garden. Ted wants us to stay overnight at the loft they're house-sitting and party with their friends, Lewis Warsh already there, still angry about the rejection letter I returned to his wife with her name for my poem titles: *Sorry but Anne Waldman is not right for THE WORLD*. Lee doesn't like that Alice is Ted's younger, second wife, the fear she has about me, so after calling Sue B in DC watching our kids, to see how they're doing, Lee wants to go home. We get in the car and I drive us back.

25

When Ted and Alice come to read at Trinity we give them our bed, where they make much noise during sex, laughing and talking, before I spend the night in a hospital after Caitlin and Miles eat old rat poison they found outside the complex's dumpster. Miles has it in his mouth when I get to him. The hospital I rush them to, I only find out later, is run by a religion that doesn't believe in blood transfusions so I wait anxiously after their stomachs are pumped to see if they'll be alright. When it's clear they will be, I go home to tell everyone that the kids are okay, and Ted shows me the new tracks on his arm where he's shot up a bunch of speed, seeming proud of it.

26

I've admitted I'm an alcoholic, but not an addict cause I hate needles. Some junkie friends seem as much into the ritual of the needle as the high. I think the hippie slogan SPEED KILLS means shooting it. I'm smoking more weed, including while Lee and our kids sleep and I can't, hiding out in the bathroom. I've snorted heroin or smoked it sprinkled on tobacco, and got so high on opium I didn't want to come back. I've taken any pill anyone offered. And now that cocaine's more available I do it more. I only did LSD and mushrooms once. Or so. Like my black friends I think hallucinogens are for crazy rich white kids who don't care about losing control of their brains. I just want to feel good.

27

Stephanie, a tall, bright, Trinity student with long red hair, starts dating the first rock critic at *THE WASHINGTON POST*, a young photographer with long hair and a beard so his editor figured he's in touch with youth culture. I take friends to see the guitarist Roy Buchanan in a Maryland road-house where he plays brilliantly improvised solos with one hand while drinking a beer with the other. Stephanie's boyfriend writes about him, leading to the veteran musician's late burst of fame. She wants to know why I'm not famous too. In Colo-rado, George Kimball helps Hunter Thompson get national publicity as the first radical/writer to run for sheriff. Two years after I did the same.

28

Angela's women's meetings radicalize Lee. I'm reading articles in alternative rags about sexism and women's lib, but a cartoon gives me my epiphany about it. A man in an easy chair reads aloud to his wife doing housework: *It says here that in the home, the man is the bourgeoisie and the woman the proletariat.* Lee's marching again, first with a few hundred women to The Pentagon, a precedent. I take the kids in the car to join her at their destination where a brave and beautiful and calm Vietnamese woman speaks as balloons are released. For the next event, Lee marches with thousands of women on the Capitol as part of a protest by women across the country.

29

The May Day 1971 demonstration is the biggest anti-war protest ever, with what seems a million people. Walking through the crowd on the National Mall, past tents some have set up, I sell copies of *RISING UP ANGRY* and hand out other papers put out for the protest. As The Beach Boys sing on the main stage, I reach what seems like the very center of this temporary city to find Gene holding a joint out to me as he explains that once again he'd just been talking about me to this pretty white hippie girl. I take him home to see Lee and the kids, folks sleeping all over our pad, including Max, a Viet Nam vet from Iowa at his first demonstration, Ken W, and a bunch of *RISING UP ANGRY* cats.

30

The May Day protest makes a lot of DC feel like a gigantic but dangerous carnival. Soldiers with fixed bayonets line Wisconsin Avenue in Georgetown where one responds with *Right on*, when we tell him we're trying to shut down the government to stop the war. When we ask another if his rifle is loaded, he says I'll trade you my bullets for some acid. The GIs are eventually withdrawn for being too friendly with protestors. The cops replacing the soldiers arrest so many so randomly, the jails quickly overflow so they use RFK stadium to put the thousands being detained, who immediately rechristen it: *SMASH THE STATE CONCENTRATION CAMP NUMBER 1.*

31

When reporters, and Congressmen and women, visit RFK stadium, the detainees sing *We all live in a concentration camp* to *YELLOW SUB-MARINE* and request Bob Hope and his USO troupe. The authorities decide to move those arrested to the DC Coliseum during the night. Before they do, Max tosses wire cutters over the fence. The soldiers ignore the hole as it's cut, except warning to watch out for lifers. Ken flees with others through the hole into the hood where street dudes promise they'll soon join these white kids in a revolution. I try to get to the microphone next day at The Justice Department protest to tell of The Great Escape but am prevented.

32

We hear that a white lady held at The Coliseum is being feted for turning seventy-one. Attorney General John Mitchell, looking like El Duce, glares down at us protestors from a window high up in the Justice Department building. In the crowd are hippies, office workers, veterans, the old, and the young. Though mostly white, there are those with darker skin as well. I watch one old pink lady chant along with the crowd: *One, two, three, four, we don't want your fuckin' war.* When police, swinging nightsticks, attack the protestors, cracking heads, arresting another several thousand, I keep one eye on the perimeter so am able to signal those with me to split just in time to avoid arrest.

33

Next day, preparing for another march on The Capital, people line up for different options like those willing to be arrested, those not, those intent on Civil Disobedience, those not. When the 71-year-old grandmother appears, having been released to avoid more bad publicity, we all sing HAPPY BIRTHDAY to her and cheer when word comes that those still held at the Coliseum have made a mock-up of The Capitol to march on in there. We set out for the real Capitol where a few Congresswomen and men, like Bella Abzug and Ron Dellums, speak from the steps as joints are passed below and a bearded blonde dude gets naked and climbs up onto the portico to cheers.

34

I watch again as cops in riot gear, their buses waiting, start making their brutal arrests and the politicians come down The Capitol steps to try and dissuade them, while a hippie cat gets hold of the microphone and starts blowing incredible blues harp. The crowd begins to chant the best slogan I've heard at any protest, and expresses the pent up feelings most of us have had since the repressive 1950s we come from: *FUCK THIS SHIT! FUCK THIS SHIT! FUCK THIS SHIT!* The cops take Polaroids to avoid the mess they made of the previous day's arrests, but the protestors are chanting and boogieing so hard they aren't still enough for the photos to work.

35

At the DC courthouse, thousands are still waiting for trials. New graffiti inside the stately building reads: *FREE THE DC 10,000!* Protestors nap, or joke with the outnumbered cops, who either joke back nervously or admit they too are beginning to doubt the war. Among the protestors are many first timers, like Max, all ready to keep going. Rennie Davis and others among the more famous Movement leaders call the protests a failure cause they don't succeed in shutting down the government, Rennie even says The Movement is over. I argue and write that it was a great success. Even Lee's and my older relatives now say Maybe you kids got it right about the war.

36

When Cal visits he tells me, away from Lee, about Bambi trying a career as a model after an agent discovered her, but the world isn't ready for a dark-skinned model, so she married a white biker from Staten Island and has more kids and now lives in The East Village. Cal says she always asks about me. He goes back to the city to tell everyone how Miles finds a cigarette butt in the sandbox and pretends to take a drag, then pass it like a joint. Roy and Karen live on the Lower East Side too now, back from three years in Africa, disillusioned with communism after witnessing Russia's and China's toxic rivalry in Africa's revolutions.

37

I make solo trips to New York, like for board meetings of The Print Center and other small press organizations I'm part of, and to visit art galleries with Peter Schejdahl, who says he considers me the best new poet out there. Most of the shows leave me cold except one of Eva Hesse's work. Peter explains she only recently died, way too young. Stunned by her biomorphic sculptural constructions, she becomes my new favorite artist. Like falling in love with a ghost. Then I run into Bambi on the street and my heart stops and resets itself as we more or less catch up. I tell her next time I'd like to meet her kids.

38

On a Midwest solo trip to score a few keys of pot to deal to friends, I meet with a poet friend in Cleveland who picks up two 18-year-olds who have some heavy Viet Nam weed. We end up stoned and coked up in a hotel room where he and one of the girls get it on in one of the beds. When the second girl pulls me into the other bed, I don't see a way out. Turns out the pot isn't the only thing from Viet Nam they have, as we discover the symptoms of an extremely virile strand of the clap Nam vets are bringing back. Lee now has confirmation that all her years of jealousy are justified. I sleep on the couch for weeks.

39

My friend's black wife says if she ever finds
the chick he got the clap from she'll cut her up.
Lee feels sad for the one I was with, certain I
took advantage of her being only 18. I explain
these young women are more experienced than
us, and into free love, like so many we know are
now, and remind Lee we've discussed having an
open marriage. But when she opens a letter from
Iowa City addressed to me, the girl's name in the
return address, and reads how she couldn't stop
flashing on me, so hitched there to discover folks
who knew of me and got my address, Lee dictates
my reply to the girl saying we shouldn't have had
sex and can't stay in touch because I'm married.

40

When they kill Black Panther George Jackson
in what seems like a set up during a breakout
from San Quentin, where they sent him after
he organized protests at Soledad Prison, it feels
like they won't stop till they kill every articulate
black political male activist on the left. The
Weather Underground and others advocate for
armed insurrection, but after the Kent State and
Jackson State deaths, there's a conflict between
those quoting Mao about how *All power comes
out of the barrel of a gun* and those saying
we've gotten too far from the love, peace, and
justice we'd been working toward. After Lee lets
me back into bed, she says she wants to move.

THE DC SONNETS

"Reduced to its skeleton, isn't our difference just this: You say, you can't change human nature; I say, it has to change otherwise there won't be any human nature."

—Walter Lowenfels (letter to Howard McCord)

1

We find a hundred-a-month rental in DC
on Emery Place, off Wisconsin in Friendship
Heights. A funky old house with an overgrown
unused greenhouse out back, a tiny front yard,
three rooms on the second floor, on the third
an attic, on the first a living room, kitchen,
dining room, and office we use as a guest
room too, with a basement apartment sublet
by a Chinese-American college kid who not
long after we move in tries to kill herself, her
parents overly apologetic when they come to
get her things. Lisa, a student of mine, rents it
next. A native of Puerto Rico, dark-eyed and
intense, she shyly comes out as a lesbian to us.

2

Dave Marcuse, a bear of a man, has a bookstore
on M Street I help him move to an old house on P,
near Dupont Circle: THE COMMUNITY BOOK
STORE. There's a large room upstairs for meetings
I talk him into letting me use for a weekly open
poetry reading series we name MASS TRANSIT.
I hope to discover local poets I can relate to, who
don't conform to academically accepted styles
but have their own original and diverse voices,
knowing there's an audience for that after seeing
the standing-room-only crowd at a reading at The
Institute for Policy Studies for the publication of
*CAMPFIRES OF THE RESISTANCE: Poetry From
The Movement*, with four poems of mine included.

3

To prevent MASS TRANSIT readings from being dominated by one person, and to help new people feel comfortable sharing their poems, the rules I come up with are: anyone can read, but not other's poems unless they're in the room, keep it short, and no criticizing what others read. The room is carpeted, the only furniture a bench, so most of us sit on the floor, a hat passed around for money for drinks and snacks. It attracts the kinds of poets I'm looking for who have their own unique voices, including Terence Winch, Bronx-born son of Irish immigrants, who also writes and plays traditional Irish music.

4

Terry moved to DC with his girlfriend, Marie, his older brother, Jesse, already in town after attending Howard University to study African drumming, one of the rare white students there. Like me, Terry is the youngest in a big Irish family whose mother has passed. He's tall, lean, and always seems to have a wise crack handy. Like walking down Wisconsin Avenue in Georgetown the first time he hits me with a smart ass bit at my expense. I stop walking. He asks why. I say If we're gonna be friends man, you can't do that, or I'll have to punch you. Fortunately, he doesn't do it again until I've learned to not take myself so seriously.

5

Trinity has an Early Childhood Development Program so I bring my kids to be cared for while I teach my classes and Lee is busy with feminist activities. I take them when I work at the bookstore too, ordering favorite tomes like LeRoi Jones's, now Amiri Baraka's, autobiographical TALES. But I challenge his politics at a public forum in DC cause he had an affair with Frank O'Hara and married Jewish poet Hettie Cohen yet regularly uses anti-gay and anti-semitic language. His poetic co-option of the police command *Up against the wall motherfucker* made him famous, even before Jefferson Airplane used it on *VOLUNTEERS*.

6

When Etheridge Knight stays with us for a poetry reading at a nearby prison, he takes me along, the only white non-convict in the audience of mostly black prisoners digging his poems. But when he talks about variations in oppression not mattering, if crushed between steel or satin you're still crushed, or how poor Africans would find the poorest black Americans well off, or how when he was in prison and his cellmate got solitary it didn't make him feel any less imprisoned, they aren't buying. Pointing to me he says how young white people could be oppressed too, like in their struggle against the war, and racism, and sexism. But most look at me like I'm a bug they just noticed and need to eradicate.

7

My artist friend Sylvia paints her letters to me on large sheets of brown paper. One day she sends one more like a banner, with huge writing spelling out LALLY SUPERSTAR. When I ask why, she says They showed *WHITEY!* in Iowa City and people say you're a movie star now. The American Film Institute, which financed it, the first feature length movie they've done that for, is headquartered in DC. At their office I'm recognized from the film. I tell them I haven't seen it, so they screen it for me and Lee, and there we are: her and baby Caitlin in our Iowa Quonset hut, my old friend Gene too, and me as a radical, more or less like myself, in a real, if flawed, film, that ends up mostly ignored.

8

Andy Grundberg, a young New York poet and photographer, visits us in DC. He and I drive up to Peekskill, New York, to meet Walter and Lillian Lowenfels. Walter was a much admired poet in the 1920s and '30s for his radical poems and politics but long since forgotten, except by old lefties, and some of us younger ones. You can see the child in the old poet's eyes every time he speaks, except when defending The Communist Party's politics and policies. We became friends through the mail after he sent me his *THOU SHALT NOT OVERKILL* and asked for poems for an anthology he ended up not including me in, explaining later, he forgot.

9

I'm behind the counter at the bookstore when a tall, white, almost preppy, young man asks for a book on New Jazz. As I lead him to it, we start a discussion on music, politics, and poetry that'll last for decades. I recognize his name, Bruce Andrews, from a short poem he has in the latest *PARIS REVIEW*. Working on a graduate degree at Johns Hopkins before leaving for more studies at Harvard, he's a fan of Robert Grenier, who I knew at Iowa, and of Ashbery's *THE TENNIS COURT OATH*, which I'm reevaluating. Bruce believes poetry should be about aspects of words other than primary meanings. Connotations over denotations. Or what I call warm-up exercises.

10

A young worker at the bookstore sends me a man my age looking for a poetry book. He's Ed Cox, a wiry Navy vet who I learn grew up poor in DC with a mother who killed herself. A mostly self-taught poet and poetry lover, he's been influenced by academics like Reed Whitmore at the nearby U of Maryland. We don't have the book, but I turn him onto ones by George Oppen and Larry Eigner, and invite him to MASS TRANSIT. Like many at the weekly readings, Ed thinks of himself as an aspiring poet cause he hasn't published many, if any, poems yet. But I tell him his poetry is already more original than Whitmore's.

11

Some of the ten thousand arrested in the May Day protests have to stay in DC for trials. Many band together to rent old houses, becoming what we call communes, named for the streets they're on, til gay men come up with more outrageous names like Skyline Faggots, or The Greta Garbage Collective. One night two guys from Skyline Faggots stop in a Country and Western bar across Wisconsin Avenue from our street and are thrown out for holding hands. They go and get the gay commune guys and return to the bar and tear the place up, even putting the bouncer in the hospital, which I read about in the next day's *WASHINGTON POST*. The first time I've ever heard of gay men doing anything like that.

12

We rent a room to Abbie, a tall, frizzy-haired, Jewish, leftie, London lawyer, whose Arab lover, half her size, raises funds for the Palestinians by renting cars to crash into other Arabs' taxis for the insurance money. The attic to Chuck and Jackie, a Jewish-afro-haired, mellow stoner, and wary, lanky, Waspy blonde Brit working as a nanny. We all take turns cooking, a first for me. I get high and walk to the market with the kids to see which veggies call out to me, add tomato sauce and spaghetti, and am happily surprised by the outcome, meals to feed two kids, several adults, and whoever's in the guest room, once a slim, long-red-haired cat rumored to be the Madison bomber, and his two Irish setters.

13

I help start THE WASHINGTON FILM CLASSROOM and run its film series in an M Street theater on Saturday mornings with flicks like *SALT OF THE EARTH*, the 1954 documentary-style feature about a New Mexico mine strike. In the division growing on the left over women's and gay rights, most argue the primary fight is for workers and black rights. But some argue women's and gay rights are equally important. After we show *ICE*, the first New-Left fiction feature film, a slight, blond-haired hippie jumps up on the stage to confront the audience as a proud gay man challenging the homophobia on the left.

14

Venceremos Brigades are groups of activists who volunteer to go to Cuba to help harvest sugar cane, as many friends have. At a community meeting upstairs at the bookshop on whether to support the brigades, gay activists argue against it, cause gay men are being imprisoned in Cuba. A lot of Movement friends have chosen to ignore that reality. A short, red-headed, tough, Irish cat from Chicago gets on my case for the way I'm leading the meeting, accusing me of a bias against gays. Frustrated, I say Hey man, I'm trying to help and not be like some men I grew up around who'd beat you up if they were here. He says Yeah well I've been beat up my whole life but not any more.

15

One local commune hosts a talk by William Hinton, author of *FANSHEN*, a book about land reform under the Communists in China. Hinton, a big white-haired American ex-farmer, lived in rural China during the revolution. I own a copy of Mao's *LITTLE RED BOOK* and here's someone who knows Mao. As Hinton speaks, the little blond-haired gay activist comes up behind me to whisper in my ear about how Hinton and Mao have it all wrong. A lot of DC's gay radicals use made-up names, like a flamboyant, tall red-head who calls himself Flambé. The little blond-haired cat is known as Total Assault.

16

Lee digs Total. Now a feminist leader, she helps organize a march on the Women's House of Detention in New York, where I used to stop on late nights to listen to family and friends of inmates yell up to them in the Village prison, Lee's photo in a national news magazine at the head of it. The authorities' response is to shut down the jail and move the women to Riker's Island, where no one can yell to them. Lee helps organize women's marches in DC too and starts a women's coffee house. She always said she stopped writing poetry cause she wrote out of sadness but then got happy being with me. But she's writing poems again and reading them most weeks at MASS TRANSIT.

17

Ed Cox comes out as gay to Lee and me. He's athletic, a Navy veteran, and grew up on the streets, yet sensitive and sincere in ways a lot of straight men aren't. But it still surprises me. Total and Lee begin working on my macho ways. He says the way I stand, like John Wayne, with my thumb hooked in my belt, or spit into the street, oppresses women and gay men. Lee objects to my using words like motherfucker and bitch, and Total the words cocksucker, fag, and even asshole, saying why should a useful part of the body be used to depict hateful people. Rita Mae Brown, a local lesbian poet, says we are strongest when we let all our defenses down.

18

What keeps me going when Lee, Total, and others tell me how my macho ways oppress women and gays is the kids, who spend most of their time with me. I watch them chant and dance with blankets over their heads, old-peasant-lady style, going so far away without leaving, in touch with a past so far gone from us, literally, their chants in made-up words, or at least unknown to the rest of us. All that matters to me is them and the world we're trying to create so they can have it better. Not materially. Humanly. When Sue B quits go-go dancing, leaves her man, cuts her hair boy-style, and comes out as a lesbian, she's not the only woman we know doing these things.

19

I read all the feminist writing I can, and through the mail befriend Robin Morgan, editor of *SISTERHOOD IS POWERFUL*, and her husband Kenneth Pitchford. I'm amazed to learn she's the actress I had a crush on, as Dagmar, the youngest child on the '50s TV show *MOMMA*. Their writing exposes straight male defenses and conditioning, and the ways straight men try to dominate others, as almost every man I know does, including me, dismissive of any opinion but his, and reveal the positive force and creative potential in feminist and gay consciousness. They convince me.

20

When Paula comes to visit with Sue, a married woman too, I realize the visit is a kind of honeymoon for them, acting on an attraction they've slowly been realizing, and am more sympathetic to them than to their unaware husbands back in the Midwest. As they talk and laugh with Lee, sharing their ideas and experiences with little acknowledgement of me, or none, I feel like I have somehow become invisible, then suddenly realize the record playing, with Aretha singing *I never loved a man the way I love you*, and Paula beaming, has a double meaning for her and her friend now. As it would for gay men too.

21

In bed alone, while Lee hangs with Paula and
her friend downstairs, I touch myself for the
first time in sensual ways, not what the priests
used to call self abuse, and discover I don't
mind how skinny I am, how soft my skin and
hair are, as women often tell me to my chagrin,
but actually dig myself as much as I do all the
women I've made love to and still want to. In
the morning my eyes in the bathroom mirror
look softer, more open and accepting. The
old standards of masculinity seem so out of
touch, literally, I write in a journal how *fem-*
inists and gay men are right, this is the rev-
olution our society needs to open the fuck up.

22

As the feminists and gay activists we know
meet strong resistance, they concentrate on
me, cause I'm open to their ideas, though
many of them contradict what I've always
thought and believed. It's stressful in ways
I've never known before. Then, one day, in
class, I'm teaching Frank O'Hara's poems
THE DAY LADY DIED and *A STEP AWAY*
FROM THEM, pointing out how artfully
they're structured, and suddenly I choke
up, tears coming to my eyes as I realize
O'Hara isn't just a unique word craftsman
but a real person whose presence I now truly
feel, not only in his poems, but in my heart.

23

DC doesn't have a Saint Patrick's Day parade so
the book store and others organize a march to
the English Embassy where an old Irish lady tells
how her brother was killed by The Black and
Tans, and Terry and Jesse sing rebel songs, and
the loudest chant is JOHN BULL BULLSHIT!
Some Trinity students show up, Ed Cox too. I'm
aware how uptight, male, and anal retentive
the leadership of the protest is, including me,
despite the Baltimore contingent accusing us of
not being militant enough, and how soft spoken
and almost effeminate an old IRA dude is, in
ways I remember young Irish immigrant men I
knew as a boy were, like one who lived with us.

24

Lee, me, two new friends, and Jim Haining, our
big, slow-talking, young, Texan, poet friend now
living in Baltimore, get into a late night stoned
discussion about the new vibes that came out
of the weekend of Paula's visit, me thinking of
the men we learned had lived in our house
before us, had grown old there together, and
after one died, the other killed himself, when,
suddenly our wall phone jumps, as if picked
up and put down again. I'm sure it's one of
them, they're here with us, or maybe only me.
I yell to them before I can think not to, grab my
head in my hands and cry, just enough to know
it's real, because I never cry. They cried me.

25

On seeing Warhol's *TRASH*, I write: *Why didn't any of the women say* Hey Joe, *so what, your hard on ain't working, get down, do it Joe, let's get with the cosmic vibes, lick it, love it, shit Joe, let's touch, who needs your pipeline anyway, we got a natural spring running all the time.* I imagine two people from the future watching it, or *THE LAST PICTURE SHOW, MIDNIGHT COWBOY,* or *CARNAL KNOWLEDGE*, with their scenes of male impotence, one turning to the other to ask *What's going on? Somebody get hurt? Oh, it was important once.* I realize the male climax is goal oriented, like a competition, instead of digging all the possibilities as women are teaching us to do.

26

When Ken McCullough, looking like the original mountain man, his lady Kathy Q, and their baby boy, Krishna, come to visit, I start a stoned discussion about the whole gay rights and feminist anti-macho thing, and end up declaring if us straight guys hate the idea of cock-sucking so much, then isn't it obviously totally demeaning to let our women do it. Though I never dug it being done to me so much. I end up turning my transcription of the argument into a poem, not implicating Ken by calling it *CONVERSATION WITH MYSELF*. I'm considered courageous by some in and out of the gay rights struggle, when I read it at protests and rallies and poetry events.

27

One morning at the bookstore a cowboy-hatted, free-school teacher, buying tons of books on yoga and spiritualism, freaks when I point out the sale on women's books, saying Oh yeah? Well they can have'em. We get into an uptight discussion of why he hates women's lib, him calling feminists: Bomb throwers at *PLAYBOY!* As he nervously smokes a cigarette, he says: I can't stand to see man any more divided by race and sex, our perspective must be cosmic! Then he turns to tell a young woman to carry the books to their van as he quotes Ramsey Clark: *We need strong men now!* I want to either hit him or explain it's okay to be weak.

28

In my movie criticism course I get to screen all kinds of films. But we have to watch *A CLOCK-WORK ORANGE* in a theater. After it, in a heavy conversation with my students, who think it's great, I admit it depressed the shit out of me with its total lack of humanity's capacity for love and tenderness, and its premise that thc future will contain the worst of the present. Stopping by the bookstore later, in the back room I ask if anyone saw it, and a woman says Yeah, what a great film. I cringe. Then Michael D, a gay man, says I thought it was the most depressing piece of shit I ever saw. I'm so relieved, him too, we hug. The first time I spontaneously hug another man.

29

At The Children's March at The Washington Monument, Coretta King is introduced as the wife of Martin Luther King Jr. rather than as an activist in her own right. I hear no feminism in her speech. Jesse Jackson has the crowd chant WE ARE BLACK, WE ARE BROWN, WE ARE BEAUTIFUL AND WE ARE PROUD, while my little children, Caitlin and Miles, pink and rosy-cheeked from the wind, chant along, beautiful too. Ed Cox appears in the crowd with some gay friends. I'm busy digging all the foxy black women, so hesitate when he moves to hug me, confusing him, and embarrassing me.

30

I remember how the gay guys I encountered in The Village intimidated me. Made me feel dumb and Jersey crude. The ones Jones/Baraka knew and loved and feared and despised. I never knew them. I wanted to, or, I wanted their respect but they intimidated me, as though I wasn't worth the time I gave myself. At a big meeting of DC feminists where Lee is a speaker, Rita Mae Brown challenges her from the floor saying Why should we listen to you when you sleep with the enemy? I dig Rita, and she seems to dig me. She once told me she had a Dixie Cup theory of lovers: Use'em and toss'em. She throws a pool party for women-into-women and dares Lee to show up. Lee does.

31

Ed Cox moves in with us. Over breakfast we talk about what it means to be a man and the whole macho thing. One morning I get him to try, with me, sitting with our legs crossed over our knees, and other non-macho poses we've never done before. I try to analyze why some black men can let a wrist go limp and still seem straight, or how Frankie Valli sings with a voice higher than a little girl's and still seems macho. And why Ed likes what I see as stilted straight white male poetry. Or why so much of Rita Mae's poetry sounds like straight old white male language too, despite her rants against our patriarchal society and system.

32

One feminist slogan is: *The personal is political.* Lee and our feminist friends keep trying to get me to open up about my feelings and encouraging me to befriend gay men. On a visit to Skyline Faggots Michael F calls me a brother effeminist. Everyone else still calls me a macho straight man. But he sees me as something other than straight and talks too of beauty chauvinism and how people tell him he isn't attractive. When he asks me to stay over I say no but feel guilty, so to make up for it, when I say goodbye and he leans in, I think to kiss me, I kiss him. It feels weird, uncomfortable, and totally wrong. And I instantly regret it. I wake up the next morning still feeling shaken and strange.

33

When attracted to women, I notice their eyes first, then their asses. Now I work hard to not objectify them, as feminists point out we men do. When I try to find an attraction toward men it's their eyes first too and then their asses if they seem feminine enough. A DC feminist hero who left her professor husband to become a taxi driver in middle age, and lives with her much younger female lover, has a 19-year-old daughter, Annie, who works with me in the bookstore and helps me understand why women loving women is revolutionary. But later she says, with a penetrating look, she isn't sure it's for her. When I pick up Lee at Sue B's I wait outside now cause no man is allowed to enter Sue's new place.

34

For an event at The University of Maryland, Ed Cox decides to read a publicly-coming-out poem. He's nervous about it, so a bunch of us go to support him. The reading is such a hit, several coeds want to talk to him after. We all sit around a table in the student union, where it is soon clear the young women assume I'm gay too, like Ed and Total and the other men there. It feels liberating in a way I've never experienced, as the coeds share their secrets with the gay men like they're all sisters. I'm flattered they don't take me for a straight man they'd act differently around. But I'm also confused by the ways they seem to be ignoring me, or treating me like a pet poodle.

35

Back at Total's to celebrate Ed's triumph,
I'm the only straight male but am treated
like I'm one of them. I feel filled with
conflicting emotions. Ed's still staying
with us, so when I leave he does too, with
Total. When we get back to Emory Place,
we hang in the kitchen trying to share with
Lee what happened that day. At one point
she becomes frustrated with my not being
able to open up. Then Total reaches out to
touch my arm, and I do. She says I've been
trying to get him to do that for eight years,
gets up, takes Ed by the hand and climbs the
stairs with him, leaving me and Total alone.

36

There is something seductive about the small,
blond, thin man. As we sit down on the edge of
the guest room bed I ask What do you guys do?
Meaning gay guys. He says softly What do you
want to do, Michael? I laugh, no woman has
ever said that to me. He makes it clear we can do
as little or as much of a variety of possibilities
as I want to. And we do, with more laughter.
Another first for me, laughing during sex. The
first revelation is touching another man. Feeling,
oddly, like touching myself but without feeling
it there, just in my hand and mind. The familiarity,
the understanding of what feels good and what
might not. Who I thought I was, now history.

Michael Lally

Poetry honors include: NYC 92nd St. Y Poetry Center's 1972 Discovery Award for *The South Orange Sonnets*; two National Endowment for the Arts Poetry Fellowships (1974 and 1981, the second attacked in Congress—the NEA accused of rewarding "pornography" for the poem "My Life"—in the first attempt to defund the NEA); 1997 PEN Oakland Josephine Miles Award for "Excellence in Literature" for *Cant Be Wrong*; 2000 American Book Award for *It's Not Nostalgia*. In 2018 *Another Way To Play: Poems 1960-2017* came out. Also worked as TV and film actor (as Michael David Lally), script writer/"doctor," editor, columnist, book reviewer for *The Village Voice* and *The Washington Post* among other publications. Writes the blog Lally's Alley on poetry, politics, movies, and other arts.